GREATEST
TRAIN JOURNEYS
OF THE WORLD

IN ASSOCIATION WITH
TIMPSON

GREATEST
TRAIN JOURNEYS
OF THE WORLD

ANTHONY LAMBERT

Published in the UK in 2015 by
Icon Books Ltd, Omnibus Business Centre,
39–41 North Road, London N7 9DP
email: info@iconbooks.com
www.iconbooks.com

Sold in the UK, Europe and Asia
by Faber & Faber Ltd, Bloomsbury House,
74–77 Great Russell Street,
London WC1B 3DA or their agents

Distributed in the UK, Europe and Asia
by Grantham Book Services, Trent Road,
Grantham NG31 7XQ

Distributed in Australia and New Zealand
by Allen & Unwin Pty Ltd,
PO Box 8500, 83 Alexander Street,
Crows Nest, NSW 2065

Distributed in South Africa by
Jonathan Ball, Office B4, The District,
41 Sir Lowry Road, Woodstock 7925

Distributed in India by Penguin Books India,
7th Floor, Infinity Tower – C, DLF Cyber City,
Gurgaon 122002, Haryana

Distributed in Canada by Publishers Group Canada,
76 Stafford Street, Unit 300
Toronto, Ontario M6J 2S1

ISBN: 978-178578-065-3
Book People edition: 978-178578-088-2

Images – see individual pictures

Typeset and designed by Simmons Pugh

Printed and bound in the UK by Clays Ltd, St Ives plc

ABOUT THE AUTHOR

Anthony Lambert has written fifteen books about railways and railway travel, including *Switzerland without a Car*, the *Insight Guide to Great Railway Journeys of Europe* and *Lambert's Railway Miscellany*. He has also written on railway journeys and travel for such publications as the *Daily Telegraph*, *The New York Times*, *The Sunday Times*, *Wanderlust* and *Orient-Express Magazine*. He was consultant editor to the nine-volume part work *The World of Trains*, and has travelled on the railways of over 55 countries. He has talked to a wide range of audiences about railways and travel, including the Royal Geographical Society, of which he is a Fellow.

CONTENTS

Africa

Asia

Australasia

The Americas

INTRODUCTION

Thousands of writers, film-makers, composers, painters and admen have recognised and celebrated the romance of the railway and train travel. Whole anthologies of railway poetry have been published. Who looks at motorways and sees anything but aesthetic blight and pollution? Once written off by politicians lacking prescience, railways have entered a second age. They are being seen as a solution to some of the problems facing an overcrowded and endangered planet, and are experiencing a remarkable increase in passengers where services are competently managed.

Railways are democratic, inclusive, outward-looking, sociable (if sometimes too much so). Who cannot recall engrossing or even life-changing conversations as a result of a chance encounter on a train? The way they transformed the interaction of people in an unprecedented way was recognised by artists who portrayed the new phenomenon in pictures, such as *The Railway Station* by William Powell Frith and *First Class – The Meeting* by Abraham Solomon. As Simon Bradley notes in *The Railways*, 'By 1900 or 1914, [Britons] were much readier than their grandparents had been to set these [social] divisions aside when the time came to travel.'

Train travel affords a vision of the world that seems so much more interesting than road journeys; somehow you hardly ever see anything interesting from a motorway. A character in one of R.C. Sherriff's novels hangs out of the train window, watching 'a hundred fascinating things'. As John Betjeman remarked, 'you need never be bored in a train'.

Train travel is liberating in the time it affords for oneself – to read, write, think, dream. Trollope designed a portable writing desk so that he could work during his innumerable train journeys when he was in the employ of the Post Office. John le Carré started writing the Smiley novels on the train between Great Missenden and London. Harry Potter was born on a train to Manchester. Even the idea for her Calcutta charity came to Mother Teresa on a train.

Robert Louis Stevenson captured the way train travel induces flights of fancy: 'while the body is borne forward in the flying chain of carriages, the thoughts alight, as the humour moves them, at unfrequented stations; they make haste up the popular alley that leads towards town, they are left behind with the signalman as, shading his eyes with his hand, he watches the long train sweep away into the golden distance.'

Eric Newby, writing about the Trans-Siberian journey before the Iron Curtain came down, put his finger on one of the most engaging attractions of train travel when he said that 'so many questions … have to remain forever unanswered when one travels by train'. Almost every scene from the window poses questions in one's mind and sets it wandering in a way unmatched by any other mode of travel.

Today few have the luxury of being able to take pleasure in slow travel, and anyway rail is generally faster than the alternatives up to 300–400 miles. In 1920 A.A. Milne thought he 'would much sooner go by *wagonlits* from Calais to Monte Carlo in twenty hours than by magic carpet in twenty seconds'.

And one senses that Sir Arthur Quiller-Couch, writing in 1944, rather enjoyed a dawdling journey he once took to see an old church: 'That we halted at every station goes without saying. Few sidings – however inconsiderable, or as might seem, fortuitous, escaped the flattery of our prolonged sojourn. We ambled, we paused, almost we dallied with the butterflies lazily afloat over the meadow-sweet and cow-parsley beside the line; we exchanged gossip with station-masters, and received the congratulations of signalmen on the extraordinary spell of fine weather. It did not matter. Three market-women, a pedlar, and a local policeman made up with me the train's complement of passengers. I gathered that their business could wait; and as for mine – well, a Norman porch is by this time accustomed to waiting.'

Quite apart from the intrinsic attractions of train travel, part of the explanation for its revival must be disenchantment with the alternatives. Except for those few able to turn left on boarding a plane, air travel, 'that agent of superficiality' as Peter Fleming put it, has lost any lustre it may have had, and the significant decline in driving-licence holders among twenty- and thirty-somethings in countries as affluent as Britain and Switzerland suggests a generation that has fallen out of love with the motor car.

This book is for those in harmony with all these sentiments and who choose to take the train whenever feasible. The choice of the 50 journeys is inevitably personal, and some may be surprised at their inclusion and disappointed by the omission of others. Some have been chosen for the stories they tell as well as the appeal of what passes by the window.

THE 50 GREATEST
TRAIN JOURNEYS

UNITED KINGDOM

TRAIN TO SKYE

At the end of one of his television series, Michael Palin was pictured heading home with a sign from the euphoniously named Kyle of Lochalsh station, the terminus opposite Skye where trains from Inverness meet the sea. To reach it, they traverse largely empty country once Dingwall is left behind, with only the occasional hamlet on the wind-swept moors.

The only centre of significant population was Strathpeffer, and the spa town came to be a textbook example of what happened when railway promoters encountered landed obduracy. Sir William MacKenzie of Coul owned large areas of land to the east on the obvious route for the line through the town. He demanded such costly works to camouflage the line that the Dingwall & Skye Railway was forced into building a northerly route bypassing the town. It entailed a steep gradient to the detriment of coal consumption and reduced the benefit of the railway to the town's prosperity.

As far as Dingwall, trains to Kyle share the same track as Wick and Thurso services (see page 21). Light and airy Inverness station is unusual in having platforms on two arms of a triangle of lines, one for trains to Aberdeen and Perth, the other for Kyle and the north. The latter almost immediately cross the River Ness, which drains the famous loch.

Slowing to walking pace, the train inches across Clachnaharry swing bridge at the northern end of Thomas

Telford's Caledonian Canal, built between 1803 and 1822. The scale of the task called for such innovations as the use of two steam bucket dredgers built by the Butterley ironworks in Derbyshire. The train skirts the waters of Beauly Firth, with the Black Isle on the far side, so named because in winter snow seldom settled there and it looked black against the surrounding white.

Past Muir of Ord, the railway joins the Conon Valley, where a new station was opened in 2013. As the train approaches Dingwall, a square stone tower erected in 1907 on Mitchell Hill comes into view; it commemorates the stonemason's son who rose through merit to become Major General Sir Hector Archibald MacDonald, who played a key role in the victory at Omdurman. A later conflict is recalled by a brass plaque on the station in tribute to the Ross & Cromarty Branch of the Red Cross Society, whose members doled out tea to 134,864 sailors and soldiers on their way to bases further north between 20 September 1915 and 12 April 1919.

Leaving Dingwall station the train crosses the short Telford-engineered Dingwall Canal and veers west away from the Far North line. A sudden turn to the north marks the site of Fodderty Junction, where a line to Strathpeffer once continued west to the spa town. Opened in 1885 after the grim reaper had carried off Sir William MacKenzie, and his son had reversed his father's opposition to the railway, the Strathpeffer branch once enjoyed through carriages from London King's Cross and later Euston. The Highland Railway was in the vanguard of railway publicity; even nabobs in Bombay were encouraged by the *Times of India* to consider Strathpeffer for their next home leave.

Forest thinning has opened up spectacular views to the west as the train grinds up to the dramatic defile of Raven's Rock and the site of Achterneed station, which for 15 years had to masquerade as the stop for Strathpeffer. Crofts around Achterneed had been given to veterans of the Highland Corps who had fought in the American War of Independence.

Delightful views across Loch Garve precede arrival at Garve station, followed by a steep climb towards the next summit at Corriemuillie and its nearby shooting lodge. Rather like the Ffestiniog Railway, the Kyle line had to be relaid at a higher level in the 1950s to allow construction of a hydro-electric project at Loch Luichart, drowning the old station of Lochluichart.

Desolate and dramatic moorland flanks the line. After the train describes a sweeping S-curve between two small lochs near Achanalt, it bowls along Strath Bran with an occasional ruined croft to recall one of the darkest episodes of Highland history when crofters were turned out of their homes to make way for sheep.

It's hard to imagine the day in 1877 when a patterned carpet of Hunting Stuart tartan was laid on the platform at Achnasheen for the arrival of Queen Victoria and her onward journey by royal carriage for a week at the Loch Maree Hotel. In the 1930s, the most complicated shunting procedure at Achnasheen took place, when restaurant cars were exchanged between The Lewisman and The Hebridean, sometimes complicated further by the presence of a goods train.

The line climbs again, past Loch Gowan, to the highest point on the line at Luib Summit at 197 metres (646 feet). A steep descent past impressive peaks and corries and the Monroe of Moruisg is followed by the sight of a beautiful wooded glen, a remnant of the Caledonian Forest, before Achnashellach. The Prince of Wales, staying at the lodge here in 1870, failed to hit one of the 500 deer driven towards his gun.

Following the River Carron, the line reaches Strathcarron station, which marks the transition from wild moorland to sea loch. For the entire 18 miles (29 kilometres) along the southern shore of Loch Carron, the train seldom ventures more than a stone's throw from the water, edged with pink sea thrift and seaweed.

For 27 years Strome Ferry was the western terminus of the line, with a pier on the loch and an overall station roof. During a weekend in 1883 an unruly congregation of Sabbatarian 'Wee Frees' physically prevented a fish train for London being loaded until midnight on the Sunday. Suppression of their protest required first a detachment of six constables to be dispatched from Dingwall followed by a much larger force, and troops on standby at Fort George.

To combat the threat to western isle traffic from the railway extension to Mallaig (see page 27), the Highland Railway with the help of a government grant decided to press on with the original plan for a terminus at Kyle of Lochalsh. The cost per mile of the 10.5 miles (17 kilometres) was five times as much as the rest of the line from Dingwall. Every foot was hard won: the railway burrows through cuttings of Torridonian sandstone, weaves in and out of coves and slices through headlands of gneiss and quartzite.

The platform of Duncraig serves Duncraig Castle, which was built in 1866 by Sir Alexander Matheson after he acquired in the Far East a fortune large enough to allow him to retire at the age of 36.

Plockton is one of the prettiest villages on the west coast and even has palms along the high street and a church by Thomas Telford. The station houses a restaurant, and the faux signal-box is a bunkhouse. In the loch near the whitewashed village is Heron Island, with its heronry among dense Scots pine; J.M. Barrie passed the island many times when travelling by train to Kyle on his way to the Outer Hebrides and it is credited with inspiring the setting for the island of the Lost Boys in *Peter Pan*.

Journey's end on the pier at Kyle has lost something since the road bridge across Kyleakin was opened in 1995, and not only the rationale behind the Skye Boat Song. But the railway holds its best views till last: where Loch Carron meets the Inner Sound, Skye's Cuillin Mountains, the Applecross peninsula and the island of Raasay form a panorama that can be literally as well as figuratively breathtaking.

How long: 2 hours 30 minutes

THE FAR NORTH

The journey from Inverness to Britain's most northerly town, Thurso, is overlooked in favour of better-known Highland lines further south. Yet from the moment the train clatters over the Caledonian Canal on leaving Inverness, the journey is full of interest and takes in some of Scotland's most beautiful scenery. In winter especially you would be unlucky not to see deer, and raptors can be seen in the Flow Country of Sutherland.

The section as far as Dingwall is shared with Kyle of Lochalsh trains (see page 16). From the junction just north of Dingwall station, the Far North line heads north-east through Easter Ross farmland, passing largely 18th-century Foulis Castle, seat of Clan Munro, to the west. The line joins the shore of Cromarty Firth, where bottlenose dolphins can be seen breaching, no longer disturbed by the flying boats

Photo: Rob Faulkner

that used the sheltered Firth as a base during the Second World War.

After passing Alness and the town's Dalmore distillery, the train arrives at Invergordon, which during the First World War was one of the three major Scottish naval bases as well as an American base for minelaying. The Highland Railway (HR) became the conduit for men and *matériel* to Invergordon and Scapa Flow in the Orkneys. From February 1917 there was a daily naval special between London Euston and Thurso with stops on the Highland at Inverness for rations, Alness and Invergordon. These trains became known as 'Jellicoe Specials' after the Admiral of the Fleet. However, the dry steam coal from the Rhondda Valley and its environs on which the fleet relied was delivered by sea from ports in southern Scotland; the volumes would have overwhelmed the largely single-track HR. Invergordon was the scene of a good-natured mutiny in 1931 following a Depression-era pay cut.

Invergordon intends to emulate the success of Chemainus in British Columbia by becoming known as 'the mural town', and the station has an example entitled 'The Long Goodbye', recalling servicemen leaving for war in 1914 and 1939.

Passengers have the last views of the Black Isle to the south as the train turns north-west at Fearn and reaches the mouth of Dornoch Firth and Scotland's oldest royal borough, Tain, which received its charter in 1066. The unstaffed station building has been converted into the Platform 1864 restaurant.

The railway climbs beside the Kyle of Sutherland, passing Bonar Bridge, whose first road bridge across the Kyle was built in 1812 following a ferry disaster that claimed 99 lives. In the woods above the station at Culrain is Carbisdale Castle, built in 1907–17 by the widow of the 3rd Duke of

Sutherland and the refuge of the Norwegian royal family during the Second World War. Subsequently a youth hostel, it was sold in 2015 to developers planning a five-star hotel.

The train crosses the Kyle on the high lattice girders of the Grade A listed Oykel Viaduct, opened in 1868, and passes Invershin station – at just 706 metres (772 yards) from Culrain station, this is one of the shortest distances between stations in Britain. The climb inland continues to Lairg, railhead and centre of sheep sales for a vast swathe of the north-west Highlands. Nowhere else in Europe can match the one-day sheep sales, and the HR devised double-deck sheep vans to increase capacity. On 17 August 1949, for example, 26,000 Cheviot sheep were sold, and as many as five trainloads would be dispatched south.

Bleak moorland scenery with few trees and the occasional whitewashed cottage pass by as the train descends Strath Fleet through Rogart back to the sea at the former junction of The Mound. Here a branch to the royal burgh of Dornoch went off across Telford's great embankment of 1813–16. The railway skirts Loch Fleet, with the Skibo Castle estate visible on the south shore. Dating from the 12th century, the castle was bought by the fabulously wealthy Andrew Carnegie in 1897 and encased in a vast baronial pile; it is now a hotel and club grand enough for Madonna's second wedding in 2000.

Golspie and Dunrobin stations are both associated with the 3rd Duke of Sutherland, whose Scottish seat was Dunrobin Castle. The contribution made by the 3rd Duke to the construction of the Far North line and economic enterprises in the region cannot be overestimated. Perhaps in penance, or at least out of a sense of righting a wrong for the Highland Clearances carried out in the name of his grandfather, the 3rd Duke spent the colossal sum of £322,064 on shares in

Highland railway schemes such as the Duke of Sutherland's Railway between Golspie and Helmsdale and the Sutherland & Caithness Railway, which built the rest of the line north to Wick and Thurso.

Moreover, the 3rd Duke was passionate about things mechanical. There are stories of him and the Prince of Wales following steam-powered fire engines to a blaze when in London, but it was on the HR that he was able to indulge himself. He had Kitson of Leeds build a tank engine, named *Dunrobin*, to operate his railway until the HR took over the line, after which the locomotive continued to be kept at Brora to haul the Duke over the 86 miles (138 kilometres) to Inverness for board meetings.

The 4th Duke inherited something of his father's partiality for mechanical matters and had a handsome tank engine built in Glasgow. Also named *Dunrobin*, it was kept in a shed at Golspie. The cab of *Dunrobin* incorporated some panels that had been removed from the earlier locomotive, on which distinguished guests continued the tradition of signing their names; they included Queen Alexandra, George V, Kaiser Wilhelm II, Edward VII and Neville Chamberlain. Also kept at Golspie was a small four-wheel day saloon to take the Duke to Inverness and other places on the HR. A much grander saloon running on bogies was built in 1899 at Wolverton in Buckinghamshire, with overnight accommodation for longer journeys south from Inverness; the coach was kept in a shed at Dunrobin station and can be admired today at the National Railway Museum in York.

Thanks to the Dukes of Sutherland, Brora had several industries, besides Britain's most northerly colliery: the 1st Duke founded the Clynelish distillery, and there was a woollen mill and a brick and tile works. The section on to Helmsdale is delightful, running beside the North Sea. The station at the fishing port of Helmsdale has been converted to provide self-catering holiday accommodation. The line again turns inland and heads up the enchanting Strath of Kildonan, scene of the most unlikely of gold rushes in 1868 and 1896. The line follows the west bank of the River Helmsdale's steep-sided valley, crossing the water to reach the lonely station at Kinbrace.

High mountains rise above the moorland as the almost treeless landscape becomes progressively wilder. In the tree-sheltered station building at Forsinard, the Royal Society for the Protection of Birds has established its Flows visitor centre with trails over the peat bogs where dipper, dunlin, golden plovers and hen harriers can be seen. During the First World War, sphagnum moss was dispatched by train from Forsinard, for use in dressing wounds.

Red deer can often be seen from the train, especially in winter, as it sets off across the most barren and desolate part of the journey, across the Flow Country. The station at Altnabreac served a lonely shooting lodge, but not until Scotscalder is there likely to be a sign of life. The train descends through Caithness's farming belt to Britain's most northerly junction, Georgemas, where passengers for Thurso get the upper hand: a separate Thurso branch train used to provide a connection, while the Wick train continued south, but the importance of Thurso rose with the creation of Dounreay nuclear power station, and today the train reverses to Thurso before retracing its steps to Georgemas and on to Wick.

Thurso was the destination of 'Jellicoes' from April 1940 as well as during the First World War. Like Lairg, Thurso has been a centre for sheep sales and generated substantial rail traffic; in a four-day sale in 1949, for example, eleven trains carrying 29,650 sheep were dispatched. Neither town would be a tourist destination but for the impressive coastline and John o' Groats, ferries to the Orkneys and Faroes, and the late Queen Mother's home at the Castle and Gardens of Mey.

How long: 4 hours

THE ROAD TO THE ISLES

Unquestionably one of the world's finest railway journeys, the line from Glasgow to Fort William and on to Mallaig traverses some of Britain's loneliest landscapes: 'a wearier looking desert man never saw' was how the hero of Robert Louis Stevenson's *Kidnapped* described Rannoch Moor. The stupendous scenery is enlivened on weekdays until early October, and at August weekends, by the bark of steam locomotives working the Jacobite Steam Train between Fort William and Mallaig.

Besides trains from Glasgow Queen Street, the line is also traversed by the Caledonian Sleeper from London Euston. There are few greater contrasts in British train travel than pulling up the covers in the dark of the Home Counties and waking up to Scottish moorland and mountains.

The journey starts under the 1880 wrought-iron roof of Glasgow Queen Street; the station was built on the site of a sandstone quarry and it still has a subterranean feel, exacerbated by the climb in tunnel and trench out of the station up a 1 in 42 gradient that was beyond the power of early steam locomotion. Consequently, until August 1909, trains had to be winched up Cowlairs Incline by stationary steam engines.

The train winds through the Glasgow suburbs, passing Singer station to remind one of the factory where almost 7,000 workers made 13,000 of the eponymous sewing machines each week, and of a time when there wasn't much that Britain didn't manufacture. Today the train passes soulless sheds simply selling stuff. The railway comes close to the Clyde at Bowling before Dumbarton and its volcanic crag and castle. There are fine views over the estuary, but little shipping disturbs its waters compared with a century ago when railway-owned paddle steamers frothed the water between many a Clyde and island pier, besides innumerable cargo ships.

The 100-mile (161-kilometre) West Highland Railway begins at Craigendoran Junction, where the train turns abruptly north along a ledge with broadening views over Gare Loch. The diesel engines growl up the bank through leafy Helensburgh, while ships ride at anchor in the estuary, before disappearing behind loch-side woods of birch and oak. Churchill departed on three of his four wartime visits to see President Roosevelt from Gare Loch's Admiralty port of Faslane.

From Garelochhead there is a spectacular view back along the narrow loch to the south before one of those almost theatrical transitions that punctuate the route. The train burrows through a fern-clad cutting and emerges to a panorama over Loch Long, where it is joined by Loch Goil. Arrochar & Tarbet station, which once supplied breakfast baskets to northbound passengers, lies between lochs Long and Lomond on a strip of land used as a portage in 1263 by King Haakon IV of Norway as he sought more places to raid.

The views along Loch Lomond are some of the finest of the journey, the railway running along a shelf cut into the hillside above a dense canopy of trees. A summer ferry links

Photo: 96tommy

Inveruglas with the idyllically situated Inversnaid Hotel on the opposite shore. Near the hotel is Rob Roy's cave, where the red-headed fugitive Jacobite, much romanticised by Sir Walter Scott, is said to have holed up. Perhaps one day the largest vessel built for a British inland waterway, the paddlesteamer *Maid of the Loch*, may again churn the loch's waters. Launched in 1953, she is moored at Balloch at the south end of the loch and welcomes visitors while fundraising continues for full restoration.

The country becomes wilder as the train starts the long climb up Glen Falloch beside the birch-fringed river. After heavy rain, not unusual hereabouts, waterfalls can be seen scoring a ribbon of white against the dark rock; this was the valley Wordsworth described as 'the vale of awful sound'. The climb ends at the meeting of three glens and the junction for Oban at Crianlarich, where the train usually divides. Though the West Highland line once boasted dining-cars, the refreshment room at Crianlarich used to dispense wicker luncheon baskets, and a tea-room still serves passing travellers.

The climb continues up a V-shaped valley to County March summit at 312 metres (1,024 feet), and snow posts on the adjacent A82 must have made many a passenger thankful they were not travelling along it. One of the most dramatic features of the railway is heralded by cone-shaped Ben Doran; the railway leaves the River Orchy to turn east into a great horseshoe curve on embankment and viaduct to reach the lower flank of the mountain and continue up Glen Orchy, sharing the valley with the river, road and an old military road now part of the West Highland Way footpath.

North of the lonely station at Bridge of Orchy, the railway passes Loch Tulla, and for the next 32 miles (51 kilometres) nothing more than a track is seen again. The wilderness of

Rannoch Moor is majestic, one of those rare places in Britain that feels truly wild, and it was home for families at some of the most remote railway postings in Britain where passing loops were created, at Gorton, Rannoch and Corrour.

For many years the two shifts at Gorton were covered by a signalman and his daughter. There was no public station there, but the early morning train stopped specially to pick up the children of railway workers living in the few cottages to take them to school at Rannoch, a timetabled station though a desolate spot in the middle of the moor made famous by Robert Louis Stevenson in *Kidnapped*. Children living in lineside cottages further north were picked up by a morning train and taken to school in Fort William. After Easter 1938, however, the school at Rannoch became overcrowded, and so the railway company set up a school at Gorton in an old railway carriage on the platform, and Argyll County Council provided a teacher from Bridge of Orchy to instruct the pupils, who once reached eleven in number.

Saplings were planted around the moorland cottages to act as windbreaks, and clumps of trees became railway landmarks in the desolate landscape. The water on Rannoch is unsafe, so the first train of the day stopped to deliver twelve buckets of water from the locomotive tender to the cottages. After dieselisation it was brought from Fort William in more hygienic containers. If emergency medical help were needed, a locomotive would take a doctor from Fort William or Tulloch. This was an unenviable assignment, because it meant running tender-first for many miles on the return journey, there being no means of turning a locomotive. Tender-first running on the West Highland was avoided at all costs, and on one occasion the three men were so chilled that the fireman could hardly hold the shovel.

When railwaymen from these places went on holiday, a rather particular breed of relief man was required: a portable bed, cooking apparatus, fishing rod and a snare wire were necessary accoutrements. Sometimes the same train delivering the relief man picked up the family he was replacing, so there was time for only a brief exchange. One man found a note for him in the kitchen detailing not railway matters but instructions on how to look after the poultry, cats, dog and three goats.

To the north west of Gorton are the remains of trenches dug by 'Butcher' Cumberland's troops during the 1745 Jacobite Rebellion. The pause at Rannoch station usually sees a few well-equipped walkers alight, enough to support a tea-room in summer and the adjacent Moor of Rannoch Hotel. At the end of the platform is a boulder with a profile of James H. Renton cut into it; capital provided by this director of the North British Railway came to the rescue when the moor was swallowing money as well as all attempts at laying a foundation on the bog. It was eventually floated on layers of turf and brushwood, using methods used by George Stephenson in crossing Chat Moss on the Liverpool & Manchester Railway in the late 1820s.

North of Rannoch station at Cruach is a shed covering the line to protect the track from drifting snow which is unique in Britain. Corrour is the summit of the line at 411 metres (1,348 feet) and shot to fame for a sequence filmed at the station in Danny Boyle's 1996 film *Trainspotting*. It was built as a private station for the estate of Sir William Stirling-Maxwell, a founder member of the National Trust for Scotland and whose wealth helped fund the building for Glasgow's Burrell Collection.

The treeless undulating peat bog continues, with lonely Loch Treig below the line to the west, until Tulloch station, which has been converted into Station Lodge bunkhouse. Turning abruptly west, the railway is joined by the road from Kingussie to Fort William. The railway follows the River Spean, which can become a foaming cataract through the Monessie Gorge.

The train passes Spean Bridge station, once the junction for Fort Augustus – a railway that entertained risible delusions of grandeur during its promotion – and descends through forest to the sea and the terminus at Fort William. Built in the shadow of Ben Nevis, Fort William was reached by the first public train in 1894, but it was 1901 before the extension on to Mallaig was opened. The locomotive depot at Fort William is home to a couple of steam locomotives during the Jacobite season, and the turntable from London Marylebone was installed here to turn them.

The Mallaig line was one of the last railways to be built during the first railway age and pioneered the use of new construction methods, introduced by 'Concrete Bob' McAlpine. Trains for Mallaig turn west past the end of long Loch Linnhe and clatter over the swing bridge at Banavie with a glimpse up the eight-lock Neptune's Staircase, the principal engineering feature on the Caledonian Canal.

The train runs right beside Loch Eil and climbs to the 21 curving spans of Glenfinnan Viaduct, which must be one of the few concrete structures to have weathered well and enhance its setting. So photogenic is it that it featured in four of the Harry Potter films as well as the Bank of Scotland £10 note. From the viaduct passengers look down on the Glenfinnan Monument, topped by a Highland chieftain, which recalls the ill-fated 1745 Jacobite uprising.

Steam locomotives work hard to reach Glenfinnan through a rock cutting that provided good building material for the viaduct. The station hosts a railway museum and a camping coach serving refreshments in summer. The climb continues through short tunnels, past the head of Loch Ailort and the landmark white church of Our Lady of the Braes, now a dwelling. Very different from Glenfinnan Viaduct's setting, but equally beautiful, is the viaduct at Loch nan Uamh. It was on this loch, the Loch of the Caves, that a hopeful Charles Edward Stuart landed from a French frigate in 1745, only to leave from the same spot 14 months later after the disaster of Culloden.

The panorama of mountains, dotted with sheep pounds and poignant remains of crofters' cottages, is soon complemented to the west by views over sea lochs towards the Small Isles of Muck, Eigg and Rum. The brilliant blue of the sea, edged with translucent emerald green, reminds some of the South Seas, further encouraged by seeing palms and subtropical plants growing under the benign influence of the Gulf Stream.

Past Arisaig, Britain's most westerly station, and after weaving through some stone cuttings, the railway cuts across the western end of Loch Morar, Europe's deepest lake at 310 metres (1,017 feet). On autumn nights, thousands of eels swim out of this loch for their extraordinary 3,000-mile (4,828-kilometre) journey to the Sargasso Sea to lay their eggs. The Station Hotel at Morar (now known as the Morar Hotel) was chosen by Arnold Bax from 1928 as an annual refuge from London where he orchestrated his compositions, notably Symphonies Nos 3–7.

Running beside beaches of white quartzite and sometimes populated by sauntering cattle, the train slows for journey's end at Mallaig station, adjacent to the fishing and ferry harbour. The railway's history is one of many subjects explored in the nearby Heritage Centre. Once Europe's principal herring port, Mallaig is for many the place to follow in the footsteps of the Young Pretender and take a boat 'over the sea to Skye'.

How long: 3 hours/1 hour 15 minutes

SETTLE & CARLISLE

No other railway in England compares with this 72.5-mile (117-kilometre) main line through the Pennines for landscapes on a majestic scale. The Settle & Carlisle (S&C) links Leeds and Carlisle, but it begins formally at Settle Junction, just south of the eponymous North Yorkshire market town, and traverses the wildest parts of northern England through landscapes that have enthralled passengers since the railway opened in 1876.

It came close to never being built, and paradoxically it was saved by closure proposals. The Midland Railway (MR) obtained Parliamentary approval to build the line as a tactical move to force the rival London & North Western Railway to be more accommodating in sharing a parallel route. When the ploy succeeded, the MR applied to abandon its proposal, but Parliament was keen to promote competition and refused. So the MR made the best of a bad job and built a superbly engineered main line laid out for express trains to make good time through the difficult country.

It was a monumental task, as passengers appreciate as they gaze over panoramic views from lofty viaducts and burrow through the hard Pennine rocks in long tunnels. They would have been denied the experience had British Rail triumphed in its 1983 closure proposal. So confident

Photo: Ultra7

was British Rail of it being granted permission to shut the line that it appointed a manager to wind it down and close it. Ironically Ron Cotton had a marketing background and did such a good job that he quadrupled passenger numbers, helped of course by the widespread adverse publicity and opposition to closure. Trains were filled with passengers alerted to this jewel of a railway. The campaign to save it was so vociferous and compelling that the S&C was reprieved in 1989 by the transport minister Michael Portillo, who has said it was the political achievement of which he is most proud. The S&C has since become busy with a mix of passenger trains, excursions – many steam-hauled – and freight.

Once upon a time, you could have had lunch aboard the Thames-Clyde and Thames-Forth expresses traversing this route, with fleecy white clouds wafting over the train to remind you of the exertion up front on the footplate. Today the trains that rattle over the line are largely hand-me-downs that have seen better days, but the views are what bring people to the railway, whether simply to watch them pass by the window or to reach the start of walks from stations en route. For the small communities served by the railway, it remains an important lifeline, especially in winter, for thankfully the roads over the hills remain tortuous and slow. So the trains carry locals on shopping trips to towns and to the start of longer journeys from Leeds and Carlisle.

The exit from Leeds is shared with trains for Morecambe and Lancaster, but even the journey through the Aire Valley is full of interest. At Saltaire trains pass within a stone's throw of Sir Titus Salt's immense mohair and alpaca mill, which was the largest factory in the world when it was built in the 1850s. Salt created a model community for his thousands of workers and was continually hiring trains to take them on excursions, either to the country for rambles or to such edifying events as London's Great Exhibition in 1851 or the Art Treasures of the United Kingdom Exhibition in Manchester in 1857, which attracted 1.3 million people in 142 days. Today the mill is home to the largest collection of Hockney paintings.

A plume of steam at Keighley marks the starting point of the Keighley & Worth Valley Railway, which winds up the valley past the home of the Brontë family at Haworth and on to the moorland terminus at Oakworth. It is still remembered for providing the locations for the 1970 film version of Edith Nesbit's *The Railway Children*, with the lump-in-the-throat scene on Oakworth station when Bobbie/Jenny Agutter meets her newly released and exonerated father.

At the isolated signal-box of Settle Junction, the railway begins an almost continuous climb for 15 miles at 1 in 100, earning the soubriquet 'Long Drag' in steam days when the fireman would be shovelling almost continuously to maintain boiler pressure. Settle is a delight – both station and town. The 1891 signal-box has been restored and opened to visitors by the Friends of the Settle–Carlisle Line, whose former chairman created an extraordinary home out of the nearby water tower, featured in Channel 4's *Restoration Man*.

Beyond the market town of Settle, the railway enters the Yorkshire Dales National Park, and well-booted walkers are likely to alight at the next station of Horton-in-Ribblesdale, intent on climbing one of the adjacent Three Peaks: Whernside, Ingleborough and jelly-mould-shaped Pen-y-ghent. The landscape becomes progressively wilder, the trees stunted and wind-blown and the dark stone-walled pasture gives way to coarse grasses on open moor. This is landscape on a grand scale, the eye constantly drawn up barren hillsides to rocky escarpments and over wild fell country known only to sheep and walkers.

During the campaign to save the line, its symbol became Ribblehead Viaduct, the gently curving arc of stone that carries the line over the hollow of Batty Moss. Its desolate setting amid the Pennine hills captures the essence of the S&C. It is so exposed that railwaymen have had to cross it on their hands and knees in the lea of the parapet during ferocious storms, and coal was even blown off firemen's shovels. The spiritual needs of the few local railwaymen and quarry workers were met by church services held in Ribblehead station's booking hall between 1880 and 1956. The stationmaster here once had to file meteorological reports to the Air Ministry, and his restored stone house can now be rented for three or seven nights.

In the dark of Blea Moor Tunnel, the line reaches the end of the long climb from Settle Junction, though not the highest point on the railway. The tunnel absorbed over a third of the £3.3 million construction cost. Lovely views down Dentdale herald arrival at England's highest station, Dent, at 350 metres (1,148 feet), where the station building has been converted into self-catering accommodation, as have the huts where workers clearing snow were billeted.

Garsdale was once the junction for a railway across the Pennines to Northallerton on the East Coast main line, but only a few terraces of solid stone houses signify that this remote place was once a busy railway community. The summit of the railway is at Ais Gill, at 356 metres (1,168 feet) the highest summit on a British main line, and the sharp-eyed will see maroon summit boards on each side of the track. The great millstone-grit flank of Wild Boar Fell overshadows the line, and it was hereabouts that the country's last wild boar was reputedly killed in 1464.

The railway drops down into the valley of the River Eden, and the coarse grasses give way to pasture, dotted with isolated small barns and tree-sheltered farms. Legend has it that an earlier fortification on the site of the ruined Pendragon Castle, beside the river, was the place where Uther Pendragon, father of King Arthur, was poisoned. As the valley sides diminish in height, passengers get a distant view of Lake District peaks to the west.

Once the county town of Westmorland, Appleby is built on a loop in the River Eden and the station is situated within walking distance. From Langwathby station, there is a walk to Long Meg and her Daughters, the second largest stone circle in the country with a diameter of 107 metres (351 feet). Dating from about 1500 BC, it comprises one large and 68 small stones, supposedly representing a mother and daughters who committed heinous acts on the Sabbath and were turned into stone.

Though journey's end is near, the line has one final flourish in the beautiful section between Lazonby and Cotehill, which has been described as the prettiest part of the Eden Valley. For several miles the river runs through a densely wooded gorge with precipitous slopes of birch and bracken dropping down to the water far below. It is best appreciated on foot, and the ancient Nunnery Walks were created near the confluence of the Eden and Groglin rivers to help walkers admire the nearby waterfalls and sandstone cliffs reaching up 61 metres (200 feet).

Armathwaite is a pleasant Cumbrian village with a four-storey pele-tower on the west bank of the River Eden. The signal-box has been restored by the Friends of the Settle–Carlisle Line. The scenery is pleasant, rather than spectacular, as the railway crosses the last pasture before the border city and Sir William Tite's imposing neo-Tudor station, appropriately known as Carlisle Citadel.

How long: 2 hours 45 minutes

BELFAST–LONDONDERRY

Northern Ireland Railways have experienced the same renaissance as railways in Britain, declines in use being significantly reversed thanks to sensible investment. At one time there was even talk of closing part of the line that Michael Palin thinks is 'one of the most beautiful rail journeys in the world'.

This railway was built from both ends: from Belfast rails reached Ballymena in 1848 and from Londonderry, Coleraine first heard a whistle in 1853, but it was 1859 before Ulster's two largest cities were linked with completion of the bridge over the River Bann at Coleraine.

Trains leave from Belfast Great Victoria Street station and pass through the striking new Belfast Central station, named not for its centrality but because it was on the Belfast Central Railway. The copper-domed Waterfront Hall is passed before the railway assumes a grandstand position on a viaduct, providing views across the port towards the Harland & Wolff shipbuilding yard, once the world's largest. Scarborough-born Edward Harland had served an apprenticeship under Robert Stephenson, while Gustav Wolff from Hamburg had trained under Joseph Whitworth in Manchester.

The *Titanic* was built in their yard, and today her tender SS *Nomadic* can be seen from the train after her remarkable rescue from Le Havre and subsequent restoration. She is open to visitors at Hamilton Dock in the Titanic Quarter. To the west is Belfast's leaning tower of Pisa, the Albert Clock, which is four feet off vertical.

The railway used to run beside Belfast Lough, but it has been distanced from the water by reclamation. The line climbs to the 1930s reinforced-concrete Bleach Green Viaducts and approaches Antrim and its mock-Tudor station building through fertile farmland.

Ballymena is rich in historical and contemporary associations, with such figures as Sir Roger Casement, Thomas Eaton who founded Canada's Eaton's department stores, Olympic Gold medallist Mary Peters and Liam Neeson.

Bascule bridges are rare on railways, and the bridge at Coleraine was the first counterpoised bascule bridge in the British Isles when it was opened in 1924, having been built by Armstrong, Whitworth of Newcastle. From Coleraine there is a branch to Portrush, serving the University of Ulster, and bus links to the World Heritage Site of the Giant's Causeway and its basalt stone columns.

Castlerock is a popular seaside village, frequented on childhood holidays by C.S. Lewis, who drew inspiration from nearby Downhill House for elements in his books, including *The Lion, the Witch and the Wardrobe.*

Shortly after Castlerock station the line passes through two tunnels created in 1845 by the 'Great Blast', when 1,633 kilograms (3,600 pounds) of gunpowder were used to remove rock. The first of the tunnels, Castlerock Tunnel, is the longest operational railway tunnel in Northern Ireland at 611 metres (668 yards).

On the basalt cliffs above is the bleak ruin of Downhill, once owned by the notorious Earl-Bishop of Derry, who spent most of his life in sybaritic living and obsessive collecting rather than administering to any flock in his charge. A glimpse, best from eastbound trains, may be had of the exquisitely designed and romantically sited Mussenden Temple, a circular belvedere built for the Earl and a precursor to Ickworth in Suffolk which he also owned.

The building at still-open Bellarena station is now self-

Photo: Milepost98

catering accommodation and is overlooked by the great cliffs of Binevenagh Mountain. At Ballykelly was one of the most bizarre railway operating regimes. In 1943 the airstrip of RAF Ballykelly had to be extended across the railway to accept larger aircraft such as B-24 Liberators for the campaign against Atlantic U-boats. The crossing was controlled by a small signal-box, and priority was given to trains over even landing aircraft unless there was an emergency.

The train runs beside the dunes and golden sands of Benone Beach beside Lough Foyle, with wonderful views across to the peninsula of Inishowen. In May 1945, Lough Foyle became the assembly point for many of the 156 surrendered U-boats; 116 were scuttled off the Irish coast under Operation Deadlight.

The railway runs alongside the River Foyle and passes underneath the longest bridge in Ireland to reach the terminus. Founded in the 6th century, Derry is Ireland's only completely walled city and the last to be built in Europe, in 1613–19. The central Diamond has a fine collection of Georgian, Victorian and Edwardian buildings, and the story of the district's railways is told at the city's Foyle Valley Railway Museum, with a 2-mile (3.2-kilometre) running line.

How long: 2 hours

THE ESK VALLEY (WHITBY–PICKERING)

Skirting the northern part of the North York Moors National Park, the Esk Valley line from Middlesbrough to Whitby links a series of delightful stone-built villages and places associated with the explorer James Cook – all four of the vessels under his command were built in Whitby. The journey is partly over Network Rail and continued behind steam over the North Yorkshire Moors Railway.

Even if you have a ticket, step into the booking hall at Middlesbrough; the 1877 hammer-beam roof resting on decorated stone corbels would not be out of place in a Gothic mansion. Leaving the former steel town past the football stadium, the skyline is dominated by the transporter bridge, which has carried people and cars across the River Tees on a cable-suspended platform since 1911.

Leafy suburbs have replaced industry by Marton station, close to Captain Cook's Birthplace Museum, and across pasture-land is the volcanic outline of Roseberry Topping and an obelisk commemorating Cook. Pine-sheltered Battersby was once busy with wagons of iron ore coming down an inclined plane from Rosedale – during the 1860s and 1870s up to 560,000 tons a year were forwarded to the blast furnaces of Teesside at a time when the North York Moors produced 40 per cent of the country's iron ore.

At the station the train reverses to head east through Eskdale to the sea, pausing at solid crow-step-gabled stations such as Castleton and Danby, the village where Henry VIII's last wife, Catherine Parr, spent her childhood. Beyond a field or two on either side of the line, agriculture gives way to steepening slopes of bracken, gorse and heather. Packhorse and monastic trails once crossed the moors, and these are often today part of long-distance footpaths. Pausing at Glaisdale, it is almost impossible to believe that the idyllic rural scene was home to an ironworks until 1876 with slag heaps so large they had to be removed by rail.

Massive retaining walls protect the line as it descends a narrow gorge to Grosmont, junction for the North Yorkshire

Photo: Nick Wise

Moors Railway and the incongruous site of another ironworks until 1891. Between Grosmont and Whitby, the line is part of the Whitby & Pickering Railway, one of England's earliest railways and engineered by no less a figure than 'the father of railways', George Stephenson. The burghers of Whitby were anxious to revive the town's fortunes, since its traditional industries of shipbuilding, whaling and alum production were in decline.

Pints are still pulled in the Angel Hotel (then the Angel Inn) on the quayside where the first meeting to discuss the idea of a railway to Pickering was held. Stephenson was asked to report on the prospects for a simple horse-drawn railway, but as so often with civil engineering projects his estimate was optimistic and it required twice his figure to build the 24 miles (39 kilometres).

The full railway opened with pomp and circumstance in 1836, when not even London and Birmingham were linked by rail. It remained an isolated horse-drawn curiosity with a rope-hauled inclined plane until 1845, when it was connected at the Pickering end to the burgeoning national network. In the same year the 'Railway King', George Hudson, bought the Whitby & Pickering for less than it cost to build and set about converting all but the inclined plane to steam traction, which took over from horses in 1847.

The diesel unit criss-crosses the Esk and descends underneath the thirteen imposing brick arches of Larpool Viaduct then slows beside the estuary to terminate in the handsome 1847 stone station, complete with porte-cochère, close to the picturesque harbour. It was at Whitby that Count Dracula leapt ashore in the guise of a wolf, in Bram Stoker's novel, and the town became famous in the 19th century for locally mined Whitby Jet, used in jewellery. The abbey where the earliest known English poet, Caedmon, served as a monk stands on cliffs above the town at the head of a stone staircase of 199 steps. One of its English Heritage guides was once asked, 'Why did they build so many ruined castles and abbeys in England?'

In a triumph of common sense, enterprise and pragmatism, North Yorkshire Moors Railway steam trains are allowed to begin their journey to Pickering from Whitby. They face a stiff climb to return to the junction at Grosmont and the start of the heritage railway. It reopened in stages between 1973 and 1975, thanks to the foresight and help of the North York Moors National Park, which realised the railway's potential for reducing traffic in the national park. Today the 18-mile (29-kilometre) railway carries over 300,000 passengers a year – more than any other heritage railway in Britain.

Pulling out of Grosmont station, the train enters a short tunnel. Beside it, the parallel smaller tunnel with crenellated portal was the original tunnel through which horses plodded, and it is now a footpath to the railway's locomotive shed and works beyond the southern portal. The area of Beck Holes was once mined for ironstone and whinstone, and today's picturesque stone cottages were built for the miners. The course of the original railway was to the west and led to the foot of the inclined plane up to Goathland, which can still be clearly seen and forms one of the area's many attractive walks.

The incline was replaced by a new conventional line in 1865, but it was briefly revived in 1872 at the expense of a Leeds locomotive builder to test engines designed for a steeply graded railway in Brazil. The course of the new line provides stirring sights and sounds from the locomotives, rising as it does at an almost continuous 1 in 49 gradient aggravated by sharp curves. It would be a dull soul that was not impressed by the stentorian barks that ring through the woods and echo off the stone retaining walls beside the line as the locomotive makes a Herculean effort to heave the train into the platform at Goathland. There's always a cluster of people at the north end of the station, watching the drama of the last half mile of climbing.

Goathland station building is the youngest on the line, dating from 1865, and has the crow-stepped gables commonly seen on North Eastern Railway stations. Behind it is a coal staithe, once a common feature for unloading coal, and at the south end is the goods shed which now serves as a café. It has been imaginatively adapted by creating seating areas inside open wagons with cut-down barrels as seats and the lavatory concealed in a van. The station also offers the once common amenity of a camping coach, which can be rented for a minimum of three nights. Camping coaches were converted from life-expired carriages and provided modestly priced holiday accommodation and increased ticket sales for the railway. The delightful period atmosphere of Goathland station encouraged its use as Hogsmeade in the Harry Potter films and as 1960s-era Aidensfield in the drama *Heartbeat.*

Goathland marks a transition from deciduous woods and fields to the open bracken- and heather-covered moorland of Newton Dale. This deep channel was gouged out by glacial meltwater in the last ice age and provides the perfect trench for the railway as it continues to climb to the summit of the line 2 miles (3.2 kilometres) after leaving Goathland. The coniferous plantations date back to a government campaign in the 1920s to reduce reliance on imported timber.

At a point just after the summit, passengers depend for their support on sheaves of heather bound in sheepskin, trees and hurdles covered in moss, for this was the only way the track could be floated across Fen Bog which is 12 metres (39 feet) deep. The area is now a nature reserve for its dragonflies and birdlife. Curving beneath the flank of Northdale Scar, the line skirts Cropton Forest to reach Newton Dale Halt, opened in 1981 to provide access to woodland walks.

High above the line are the ruins of Skelton Tower, built as a lodge in 1850 by the Rev. Robert Skelton, who used it to write sermons or enjoy a quiet drink, depending who you believe. A mile before Levisham station is the Grange, formerly the Raindale Inn, where the gravity run from Goathland came to an end, and horses were taken off the 'dandy cart' in which they had been riding and attached to the front of the coach, while passengers had a drink in the pub.

Remote Levisham station also has a camping coach as well as Britain's only artist-in-residence on a heritage railway, whose studio is open to visitors when trains are running. Once through Levisham station, the line is straight for 2 miles (3.2 kilometres) before wending through more woods and past the ruins of Pickering's 13th-century castle and a trout farm to arrive at the town's attractive station. It was once sufficiently busy to warrant a W.H. Smith bookstall on the up platform, and in 2011 the station regained the overall roof it had lost in 1952.

How long: 1 hour 30 minutes + 1 hour 30 minutes

FFESTINIOG AND WELSH HIGHLAND RAILWAYS

In 2011, a remarkable project was completed when passenger trains began running over the Welsh Highland Railway between Caernarfon and Porthmadog for the first time since 1937. It would never have happened without the generosity, perseverance and skills of various individuals, as well as several pots of Welsh, European and lottery money.

In common with most heritage railways, the Welsh Highland Railway makes a huge contribution to the economic vitality of the region, but coupled with the parent Ffestiniog Railway it also provides a public transport alternative for those content with slow travel – walkers up Snowdon among them. Besides a certain lack of speed, the railway offers traditional as well as more comfortable modern coaches for those keen to experience early railway travel conditions – the Festiniog Railway introduced the world's first bogie carriages in the 1860s and some have been restored. Or one can travel in carriage no. 16, which had a compartment specially reserved for David Lloyd George when he was a lawyer in Blaenau Ffestiniog, before becoming Prime Minister in 1916. On special days there is even the chance to be hauled by one of the world's four oldest narrow-gauge steam locomotives, all on the Festiniog.

The two railways are managed jointly and share a station in the slate port of Porthmadog at one end of the Cob across the tidal estuary of Traeth Mawr. The Cob was built as part of a project devised by William Madocks, MP for Boston, to complete the reclamation of Traeth Mawr, which had begun in 1770. It took from 1808 to 1812 to build the massive stone-lined embankment across which the Festiniog Railway ran from 1836 on its winding way to the slate quarries of Blaenau Ffestiniog.

It is a spectacular start to the 13.5-mile (21.7-kilometre) journey, passengers having the sea on one side and a splendid view inland across the polder towards Snowdonia. At the end of the Cob, the train curves sharply past Boston Lodge Works, where locomotives and carriages are restored, built and maintained. Minffordd is the first station and an interchange with Arriva Trains Wales services between Shrewsbury and Pwllheli (see page 61). It is the closest station for Portmeirion, the extraordinary Italianate village inspired by Portofino that Sir Clough Williams-Ellis created from 1925 using architecturally fine re-erected buildings that he had saved from oblivion. It was a suitably 'other world' setting for the cult 1960s television series, *The Prisoner.*

Climbing past the village of Penrhyn, views open up over the valley of the River Dwyryd before the train crosses a high stone-faced embankment. Hugging the contours of the hills through the woods, the train winds around Llyn Mair to reach Tan-y-Bwlch station, where Bessie Jones became probably the most frequently photographed railway official in Britain. In 1929 she married a Festiniog Railway porter at Tan-y-Bwlch, where they lived in the station house until their retirement in 1968. In the 1930s Bessie became stationmistress and made a point of meeting all trains dressed in Welsh national costume, until the railway closed in mid-September 1939. When the preservationists reopened the line to Tan-y-Bwlch in 1958, Bessie resumed her work as stationmistress.

Down the road from the station is the Oakeley Arms Hotel, which in February 1870 welcomed a Commission from Imperial Russia that had come to see the railway. Snowdonia was the unlikely setting for a remarkable demonstration of new technology, attracting visitors from around the world when international travel was slow and difficult. The occasion was the first public display of a locomotive designed using the principles of a patent granted to Robert Fairlie in 1864, for an articulated locomotive with two sets of wheels and motion. The locomotive, No. 7 *Little Wonder,* had been built by Fairlie's father-in-law George England at the Hatcham Ironworks in New Cross, London, for the Festiniog Railway.

Photo: fairlightworks

Fairlie had a well-developed sense of the importance of good public relations and arranged with the Festiniog Railway's progressive manager, Charles Spooner, for comparative trials between *Little Wonder* and previous tank engines built by England for the Festiniog Railway.

The trials were attended by the 3rd Duke of Sutherland and the Russian delegation headed by the Minister of Transport Count Alekseyevich Bobrinskoy, as well as engineers from France, Germany, Hungary, India, Mexico, Norway, Sweden and Switzerland. The trials showed the overwhelming superiority of Fairlie's concept. On the 12th, Spooner gave a paper in the Oakeley Arms Hotel, where many of the delegates were staying; he outlined the benefits of combining a narrow gauge with Fairlie's patent locomotive. Spooner gained a gold medal from the Tsar, and Fairlie won locomotive orders from Russia, Chile, France and Sweden.

The following year the Festiniog was visited by General William Jackson Palmer while on his honeymoon. He had set up the Denver & Rio Grande Railway in the USA the previous year, and the visit convinced him of the advantages of the narrow gauge, encouraging him to settle for the 914-mm (3-foot) gauge that became so common for secondary systems in the USA.

Extensive views open up to the east towards the Moelwyn Mountains and the defunct power station at Trawsfynydd. At Ddault is a feature unique in Britain: a spiral to gain height above the waters of Tanygrisiau Reservoir, which flooded the old route and necessitated construction of a deviation, almost entirely built by volunteer labour in the 1970s. After Moelwyn Tunnel, the line descends to Tanygrisiau and fine views looking back over the reservoir before arrival at Blaenau Ffestiniog station and a cross-platform interchange for Arriva Trains Wales services to Llandudno Junction.

The 25-mile (40-kilometre) Welsh Highland Railway offers a very different perspective of Snowdonia as well as a departure from the Ffestiniog in its motive power. It is operated by a fleet of mostly Manchester-built Garratt articulated locomotives, all repatriated from South African Railways bar a single example from Tasmania. These powerful machines are ideal for the railway's sharp curves, steep gradients and heavy trains.

Leaving Porthmadog, it crosses the high street and slips out of the town behind the backs of houses and industrial buildings before the unique flat crossing, in Britain, of standard- and narrow-gauge lines at Gelert's Farm. Wide views over cow-studded fields reclaimed from the sea precede the climb past the site of Nantmor station and through a rock cutting to the spectacular Aberglaslyn Pass, voted Britain's most beautiful place by National Trust members. The railway is on a shelf high above the river in a narrow, densely wooded valley and burrows through three tunnels, the longest at 280 metres (919 feet). Swinging across the Bryn-y-Felin truss bridge the locomotive barks up the final stretch into the principal intermediate station of Beddgelert, where trains often cross.

The railway describes two tortuous S-curves after leaving Beddgelert, alternately in the shade of mossy cuttings and then in the woods of larch, oak and conifers that flank much of the railway, throwing back the sound of the Garratt working flat out to heave its train to the summit just before the next station at Rhyd Dhu. By then the forest has been left behind to give fabulous views of Snowdon to the east and across the waters of Llyn-y-Gader to the west.

In common with all the stations, there are delightful walks from Rhyd Dhu, one to the remains of quarries around Nantlle as well as a favoured route up Snowdon. Even with the hills veiled in an eiderdown of cloud, it is easy to be captivated by the landscape as Turner evidently was when he stopped to paint Llyn Cwellyn in 1798. The hillside is scarred by slate workings as the train descends a rare long straight past the neo-Romanesque church of Betws Garmon to Waunfawr station, where locomotives can take on water. It was from a radio station in the village that Marconi sent the first radio transmission to Australia, a story told in the village museum.

After Waunfawr, the railway joins the valley of the Afon Gwyrfai and follows the tree-lined river to farmland and Tryfan Junction station, where the Welsh Highland once met the now-closed standard-gauge branch line between Afon Wen and Carnarvon. Large buildings accommodate the main workshop, engine and carriage sheds.

The railway shares the old track formation with a cycle path to the quayside at Caernarfon and the lofty stone walls and polygonal towers of the castle, built by Edward I to impose his authority on the region.

How long: 1 hour 15 minutes/2 hours 30 minutes

THE HEART OF WALES LINE (SHREWSBURY– SWANSEA)

The train between Shrewsbury and Swansea wends through some of the most unspoilt scenery in the Welsh Marches and Wales, the countryside of A.E. Housman and Mary Webb. It links small Welsh towns that once hosted thriving spas served by through carriages from London Euston, such as Llangammarch Wells. There are spectacular views for most of the way, and some of the stations are bright with flower-beds and hanging baskets, looked after by local volunteers.

The line is a near-miraculous survivor, one of few remaining cross-country lines built to serve small market towns and sleepy villages and the largely agricultural activities that sustained them. Most were closed, often by malign and underhand accounting methods, during the 1950s and 1960s when government and management colluded in their extermination, to the continuing regret of their communities. The places served by the Heart of Wales line cherish their railway and help to promote its use by residents and tourists.

Shrewsbury station has a magnificent three-storey grey stone mock-Tudor façade of 1903–4, closely following the original of 1848 and looking more like a university college than a railway station. As the train begins its 122-mile (196-kilometre) journey, it passes the world's largest operating mechanical signal-box; the 1902-built Severn Bridge Junction signal-box has 180 levers and, like the station, is listed Grade II.

Cantering along the main line to Newport, to the east is the distinctive volcanic outline of The Wrekin, which has an Iron Age hill fort on its summit. The Long Mynd towers over Church Stretton, while to the east is Wenlock Edge, which inspired Housman's poem 'On Wenlock Edge …' and Vaughan Williams's eponymous song cycle. The junction of Craven Arms marks the start of the long single line of the Central Wales Railway – the Heart of Wales is a recent marketing name. To the west leaving Craven Arms is a quintessential fortified manor house; 13th-century Stokesay Castle is a series of contrasting buildings in mellow stone and has been an attraction since an unusually sensitive Victorian restoration and subsequent formal opening in 1908.

Sparsely populated rolling hills of pasture and deciduous and coniferous forest flank the line before the border town of Knighton and its ornately decorated station. The 8th-century earthwork of Offa's Dyke parallels the line. If a stop is requested at Knucklas station, passengers have longer to admire the magnificent 13-arch Knucklas Viaduct with its crenellated turrets at each end. In 1925 a fox was cornered on the viaduct by the local hunt; encountering a gang of permanent-way men on the bridge, it leapt the parapet to its death 75 feet below, but the workmen commemorated its fate by scoring 'fox' into the stonework.

A stiff climb through rock cuttings lifts the line to its summit at Llangunllo (299 metres/981 feet above sea level) before dropping down to the flower-filled stations at Dolau and Pen-y-Bont. Llandrindod Wells's hulking 19th-century hotels, such as the Commodore and Metropole, the latter's rendered walls bizarrely painted a pine-green colour, recall the town's Victorian and Edwardian heyday when 80,000 visitors a year would come to take the waters here. The fine Victorian buildings and artificial lake reflect its status as Wales's most important inland spa. In spring so many thousands of toads and frogs use the lake to mate that the road around it has to be closed.

Builth Road was one of those extraordinary remote country junctions where two lines crossed and connected, and passengers changing between them were even served by a refreshment room. Until 1962, the other equally scenic line meandered south from another isolated mid-Wales junction at Moat Lane and continued south from Builth Road to Brecon.

After crossing the River Wye, the train pauses at Cilmeri where a monument can be seen marking the reputed spot where the last indigenous prince of Wales, Llywelyn the

Last, was killed in a skirmish with an English force in 1282. In 1912, the Kaiser and his family came to Llangammarch Wells, travelling incognito; the Prince and Princess Münster were expected rather than the Kaiser, as the booking was made in those names. They must have had cardiac or rheumatic complaints, for which the spa's unique offer of barium chloride drinks and baths were recommended. The still-open Lake Country House Hotel where the Kaiser stayed had 2,000 acres of grounds offering shooting, lake fishing, tennis, golf, croquet and bowls.

If bog snorkelling or other 'off the wall' events sound appealing, Llanwrtyd Wells is the place for you. Besides claiming to be the smallest town in Britain, the former spa has carved out a new niche offering wacky as well as more conventional outdoor activities. The town's Cambrian Woollen Mill dates from the 1820s and was reopened during the First World War to employ men disabled by injuries; it still produces items made of Welsh woollen tweed.

Wild moorland scenery provides a suitable setting for the climb to the 914-metre-long (1,000-yard) Sugar Loaf Tunnel, which takes its name from the conical mounds in which the carbohydrate used to be sold. The train emerges on a shelf in the hillside with dramatic views to the south towards the Brecon Beacons and Black Mountains as the line drops steeply down to cross the gently curved eighteen sandstone arches of Cynghordy Viaduct.

George Borrow in his 1860s travels around Wales thought Llandovery 'about the pleasantest little town in which I have halted in the course of my wanderings', and its market square is still lined with 17th-century and Georgian buildings. The train now races along the flat valley of the River Tywi towards Llandeilo, where staff from the refreshment room once supplied passengers with on-train sustenance and supplied northbound passengers with footmuffs. A mile to the west is Dinefwr Park, landscaped by 'Capability' Brown and still home to fallow deer and a herd of the long-horned white cattle which have been there for over a thousand years.

Pasture gives way to signs of former industry and mining of anthracite around Ammanford, but more soothing sights for the eye return after Pontarddulais as the train runs beside the Loughor Estuary. Salmon and sea trout from the river used to be carried on ponies to Swansea market, but today the estuary is best known for the cockles that have been collected there since Roman times. At Llanelli, trains reverse and retrace the rails to reach journey's end at Swansea.

How long: 4 hours

THE CAMBRIAN COAST (SHREWSBURY– ABERYSTWYTH/PWLLHELI)

Long gone are the days when you could board the Cambrian Coast Express at London Paddington and enjoy lunch in the restaurant car that went as far as Shrewsbury. Introduced in 1927, the train called at Leamington Spa, Birmingham Snow Hill, Wolverhampton Low Level and Shrewsbury, where locomotives were changed for the weight-restricted Cambrian line. The train then stopped at Welshpool, Machynlleth, Dovey Junction and Borth, before arriving at Aberystwyth after a 5-hour 30-minute journey. After the train's post-war reintroduction in 1951, there were also through carriages to Pwllheli.

Today's passengers will struggle to find an echo of the Cambrian Coast Express's glamour in the utilitarian diesel trains that operate the line, but the glorious unspoilt landscapes more than compensate. The deep sheep-farming valleys of the inland section are redolent of the poems of R.S. Thomas, and Dovey Junction is the start of perhaps the finest stretch of coastal railway in Britain, a rollercoaster ride between high cliff ledges and beaches that affords magnificent views along Cardigan Bay. It also provides interchanges with four of Wales's narrow-gauge railways and access to another two.

Leaving Shrewsbury, the train passes close to the red-sandstone abbey church of the Holy Cross, once part of a Benedictine monastery founded in 1083. The line soon crosses the Welsh border into Powys to reach the first stop at Welshpool, where the station area is a textbook case of abominable transport planning. The imposing French Gothic building that was once the station has been separated from the railway by a brashly sited dual carriageway road. Passengers have to make do with a minimalist affair and put up with the noise and fumes of traffic, while the old station has been given over to shops.

The station was once the start of the narrow-gauge Welshpool & Llanfair Light Railway, whose Manchester-built tanks whistled their way across the town's streets and along the backs of houses to thread along the Banwy Valley to Llanfair Caereinion. Today you have to walk a mile to the start of the preserved railway on Raven Square.

There is no longer a station serving the former county town of Montgomery, and the next stop is Newtown, once known for its flannel and textile industries. Appropriately it was the birthplace in 1771 of the utopian socialist and reformer Robert Owen, whose legacy is the planned

Photo: Phil Sangwell

settlement and mills of New Lanark, today an outstanding museum of industrial history in a sylvan setting on the River Clyde. Murals created by local schoolchildren in Newtown station commemorate the association, and the town still has textile links through a Laura Ashley factory.

Moat Lane Junction was once the junction for the enchanting Mid-Wales line to Builth Wells and Brecon, but there is no sign of the engine shed that became a ballroom lit by Chinese lanterns for the wedding of a railway manager's daughter. He was in charge of the Van Railway that ran from the next stop at Caersws, where the flowerbeds are often a mass of colour.

From Caersws the train climbs to the summit cutting at Talerddig among forested mountains. The cutting at Talerddig is a defile 120 feet (37 metres) deep through solid rock and is said to have been the deepest in the world when constructed in the 1860s. It is a tribute to one of the great Welsh builders of railways, David Davies of Llandinam. It was profits from his contracts that enabled his two granddaughters to create the exceptional collection of French Impressionists now in the National Museum of Wales in Cardiff. Stone from the cutting was used to build bridges such as the fine viaduct over the Twymyn stream near Cemmaes Road.

The line drops down a wooded embankment at even steeper grades to the seat of Owain Glyndŵr's 1404 parliament at Machynlleth. The late medieval building on the site was given to the town by David Davies's grandson and is now the Owain Glyndŵr Centre.

In the middle of a marshy estuary is one of the loneliest junctions in Britain. Dovey or Dyfi Junction is accessible only by footpath and train and is where one line turns south to Aberystwyth and a northerly route begins one of the longest railway coastal panoramas in Britain, often perched high on the cliffs overlooking Cardigan Bay, to reach Pwllheli.

The train to Aberystwyth pauses only at Borth, where there is a community-run museum in the station, before the Vale of Rheidol Railway comes into view to the south. This narrow-gauge steam railway – Wales is blessed with quite a lot of them – winds into the hills to Devil's Bridge and delightful walks to waterfalls. The Great Western Railway worked hard to promote Aberystwyth, rather optimistically incorporating a dance floor for *thé dansant* when it rebuilt the station in 1925.

Much more spectacular is the northern branch from Dovey. The train soon joins the sea at the mouth of the estuary, and at low tide the sand looks as though it has been scoured with a giant butter curler to create parallel bars of gently contoured sand, probed by waders for food. The hills rise from the shore, forcing the railway along a sinuous course punctuated by short tunnels and rock cuttings. Penhelig is reminiscent of the villages linked by train along the Ligurian coast south of Genoa; the delightful jumble of tightly packed colour-washed houses is squeezed between the steep hill and the sea, seen in snapshots between tunnels.

With the coming of the railway, Aberdyfi, once Aberdovey, morphed from a small port to a small resort for golfers and sailors. The hills recede briefly as the train pauses at Tywyn, where Britain's first heritage railway, the Talyllyn, heads inland to slate quarries at Abergynolwyn. The railway was saved by a group of largely Midlands enthusiasts following a landmark meeting in the Imperial Hotel in Birmingham in October 1950.

The hills return near Tonfanau as an almost sheer cliff, forcing the railway on to a ledge so precarious that a landslip on New Year's Day in 1883 derailed the evening train from

Machynlleth. The carriages teetered on the edge, but the locomotive and its crew were broken on the rocks below. Fifty years later another accident at the same spot prompted construction of an avalanche shelter that still protects the railway.

There is little evidence that Barmouth Junction/Morfa Mawddach ever existed, but it was once a major interchange for trains heading east through Dolgellau to Llangollen and Ruabon. It even had a camping coach or two in a bay platform; these were provided by some railway companies as inexpensive self-contained holiday accommodation. The proximity to the sea caused occasional difficulties: in one storm, staff and passengers were marooned all night in the station building as water lapped the platforms, while cattle and sheep from surrounding fields sought shelter under the canopies.

The sound of the wheels on the rails becomes hollow as the train eases across the wooden bridge over the Mawddach Estuary. Over the decades, the bridge has required extensive work to save it from the scourge of wooden-hulled ships, *Teredo navalis*, the wood-boring worm. It has a cycle- and footpath that gives Barmouth an esplanade with magnificent views across Snowdonia – George Borrow said it was 'the finest sight in all Wales'. Incredibly Gwynedd County Council is considering shutting the bridge path to save money, despite it being on the Lôn Las Cymru cycle route and the Wales Coast Path, which opened in 2012, making Wales the world's first country to have a footpath around its entire coastline.

On the hillside above Barmouth is Dinas Oleu, the very first parcel of land given to the infant National Trust in 1895. Alight at the tiny halt of Llandanwg and you can walk over the dunes to the church of St Tanwg, which dates partly from the 13th century with two older inscribed stones believed to be 5th century.

The imposing hilltop citadel of Harlech Castle comes into view to the north. The late 13th-century castle built by the great fortress builder, Edward I, fell to Owain Glyndŵr in 1404, but it is the siege of 1468 during the Wars of the Roses that is commemorated in the song 'Men of Harlech'. Lyrics and music first appeared in print about 1830, being adopted as a regimental march and famously used in the 1964 film *Zulu*.

Glimpses of the headland on which Portmeirion stands can be had as the train curves west towards Minffordd; the magical 'home for fallen buildings', as its creator, Clough Williams-Ellis, described Portmeirion, is another place on the Cambrian coast redolent of Italy, with its soaring campanile and colour-washed buildings. Opened in 1926, Noël Coward came here in 1941 to write *Blithe Spirit*, and the mix of hotel and self-catering accommodation was used as a surreal setting for *The Prisoner*.

At Minffordd the train dives underneath the Ffestiniog Railway (see page 51) and passes the siding where slate was once transferred from narrow- to standard-gauge wagons. In the distance, at the mouth of the Afon Glaslyn Estuary, is the embankment used by the Ffestiniog Railway, which the Pwllheli train crosses on the level just before Porthmadog station.

Another castle, but one built by Llywelyn the Great rather than Edward, is passed at Criccieth, standing on a small hill right beside the sea. The early 13th-century stronghold frequently changed hands, relying on supplies from Ireland when under English control until its final siege in 1404 when French warships prevented access.

From journey's end at Pwllheli station, there is an arc of sand stretching towards the Llŷn Peninsula and its pretty villages within an Area of Outstanding Natural Beauty.

How long: 4 hours

LONDON–PENZANCE

The delights of the West Country have been served by crack trains since 1897, when the Cornishman from London to Penzance was introduced, gaining the distinction of being the world's longest non-stop run for the 194 miles (312 kilometres) between Paddington and Exeter (St David's), covered in 223 minutes at an average speed of 52 mph (84 km/h). New locomotives allowed the train to run non-stop to Plymouth from 1904, a distance of 245 miles (394 kilometres). The train of chocolate and cream carriages was renamed the Cornish Riviera Express in the 1920s, becoming perhaps the named train most associated with golden beaches, sea air and holidays since it served eight West Country resorts.

Its departure station would be gratifyingly familiar to its creators, Isambard Kingdom Brunel and Matthew Digby Wyatt. Paddington was completed in 1854 and designed 'after my own fancy', as Brunel put it. With the addition of a sympathetically designed fourth roof span in 1906–15, it has stood the test of time remarkably well. Passengers with time to spare before a departure can wander over to Platform 1 to admire one of the most distinguished of First World War memorials: the 'tommy' reading a letter, poignant yet dignified and resolute, sculpted as the Great Western Railway's war memorial by Charles Jagger, best known for the Royal Artillery Memorial at Hyde Park Corner.

No railway is more identified with its creator than the line to the west from Paddington. Brunel's main line was so superbly engineered to minimise gradients that it became known as 'Brunel's billiard table' and allowed it to become host to the world's fastest train, the Cheltenham Flyer, which from 1932 averaged 71.3 mph (114.7 km/h) over the section of 77.3 miles (124.3 kilometres) between Swindon and Paddington.

Today the journey can still be made in style, enjoying a Pullman service with food cooked on board and served using proper napery, branded china and cutlery, thanks to train operator Great Western Railway's improvements.

A mile or two from Paddington lies the former pig-farming district of Old Oak Common, where the original Great Western Railway had its largest depot and which may become a major station and regenerative hub on HS2 (High Speed 2, the planned railway from London to points north). From 1842–3, this section of line to Slough was paralleled by the first wires for Wheatstone and Cooke's Electric Magnetic Telegraph, which came to public attention through the time-honoured medium of crime. On New Year's Day 1845, John Tawell poisoned a woman in Slough with a glass of stout laced with cyanide of potash. Her screams of pain caused Tawell to be seen leaving the scene of the crime, as he made his escape for London. His description 'in the garb of a kwaker' (for some reason, j and q were not included in the letter code) was telegraphed to Paddington, where he was followed and arrested the next day.

It was also at Slough that the first royal train journey began, on 13 June 1842, when Queen Victoria entrained there for Paddington (the Windsor branch was not opened until 1849). Brunel and the Great Western Railway's 'Superintendent of Locomotive Engines' Daniel Gooch, who had been appointed to the position at the age of 21, were on the footplate of the almost new locomotive *Phlegethon*. They were joined by the Queen's coachman, who could not be convinced that Her Majesty would be safe without his

I.K.BRUNEL

ENGINEER
1859

Photo: Nilfanion

presence on the footplate. The next day the Queen wrote to her uncle Leopold, King of the Belgians, that she had come by 'the railroad … free from dust and crowd and heat' and that she was 'quite charmed with it'.

Meadows alongside the Thames flank the line through Burnham and Taplow to Maidenhead, where the line crosses the river by the bridge made famous by Turner in his 1844 painting *Rain, Steam, and Speed.* The debate about whether a smudge of paint is a hare and if so what Turner meant by it, gives a new dimension to the expression, setting a hare running.

The train flashes through the 2-mile-long (3.2-kilometre) Sonning Cutting, which reaches a maximum depth of 18 metres (59 feet) and was dug by 1,220 men using spades and wheelbarrows, supplemented by two steam locomotives and 196 horses. The railway rejoins the Thames before Reading station, rebuilt and enlarged by additional platforms and flyovers in 2011–15. It was during a change of trains at Reading in December 1919 that T.E. Lawrence misplaced his briefcase containing the draft of *Seven Pillars of Wisdom*; its loss and a plea for its return was published in national newspapers, without response. His feelings at the loss of an estimated 250,000 words can be imagined.

Just west of the station the train turns south-west, taking what has become known as the Berks and Hants, which became the principal route of the Cornish Riviera Express, and expresses for Devon and Cornwall in 1906 with the completion of the final missing link between Reading and Taunton. Previously trains for the West Country had travelled via Bristol so the opening ended justification for the taunt that GWR stood for 'Great Way Round'.

Beyond Theale the railway comes alongside the Kennet & Avon Canal on the south side and follows it through

Newbury – where the racecourse opened in 1905 and has its own station for race days – and almost to Pewsey. The canal moves to the north side of the line by a tunnel under the railway at Savernake, close to the site of Wolf Hall where Henry VIII's third wife, Jane Seymour, grew up. The canal links Bristol with the River Thames at Reading and took from 1718 to 1810 to complete.

A glimpse of the 18th-century chalk Westbury White Horse to the south heralds the approach to the major junction of Westbury on the edge of Salisbury Plain. Once through the Somerset hills, the train calls at the Somerset county town of Taunton and passes the junction with the heritage West Somerset Railway. The section of line on the climb up to the summit and tunnel of Whiteball was where, in 1904, the now preserved locomotive *City of Truro* is thought to have become the first engine to reach 100 mph (161 km/h) on the descent.

South of Tiverton Parkway station, the line is often prone to flooding from the waters of the Culm and Exe rivers on the approach to Cowley Bridge Junction, where the Barnstaple line comes in shortly before Devon's county town. It was at Exeter St David's station in 1934 that the idea for Penguin Books came to Allen Lane as he waited for a train after visiting Agatha Christie. He found nothing worth reading on the bookstall, and the idea for inexpensive books in paper covers at 6d (2½p) was born.

The railway between Exeter and Newton Abbot is justly one of the most admired and captivating stretches of line in Britain: it begins with views across the Exe Estuary to Topsham and Lympstone, and passes to the west the deer-park of Powderham Castle and the tiny harbour at Cockwood. Beside Starcross station is the Italianate sandstone building that once housed a stationary steam engine, part of Brunel's disastrous atmospheric system, which began operation in 1847. Creating a vacuum in front of a piston in a continuous tube beneath the track was intended to obviate the need for locomotive haulage and overcome the fierce gradients west of Newton Abbot. For various technical reasons, the system proved a failure and the atmospheric system was abandoned after 361 days.

After Dawlish Warren comes several miles right beside the sea, except where the line burrows through five tunnels. The views from the train have delighted passengers for over 170 years, but it has been the despair of the engineers charged with its maintenance. Many passengers have had a soaking when a wave crashed through a window left open, and breaches have periodically interrupted services, most recently in 2014 when the line was closed for two months after Dawlish took a battering. The impact on the economy of Devon and Cornwall was so severe that studies are being made for alternatives: an entirely new route through the Haldon Hills or, more practically, the reopening of the line across Dartmoor between Okehampton and Plymouth.

Emerging from Parson's Tunnel, the railway runs right beside the sea wall, with a popular walkway alongside. From Teignmouth the line follows the Teign Estuary to pass another racecourse just before Newton Abbot. At Aller Junction, the line to the resorts of Torquay and Paignton continues south, while the main line turns abruptly west to tackle the first of the challenging climbs through the steep hills and woods that lie south of Dartmoor. The steep gradients to the summits of Dainton and Wrangaton required pilot or banking locomotives in steam days and attracted many photographers for the spectacle of locomotives working to their limit. To the north are the foothills of Dartmoor with occasional traces of the mineral workings that spawned many tramways, most historically the Haytor Granite Tramway whose upper section has been designated an Ancient Monument.

The approach to Plymouth skirts the park of the National Trust's house at Saltram and the Plym Estuary. The naval dockyards at Devonport can still be glimpsed from the train as Plymouth is left behind, but the great excitement is the crossing of the Tamar Estuary by the Royal Albert Bridge, Brunel's greatest structure and his last. The Admiralty required a headway of 30.5 metres (100 feet), and Brunel originally envisaged a single span of 305 metres (1,000 feet), but under the financial stringency of the Cornwall Railway the design was altered to two spans. The difficulty of reaching rock through sand and mud for the central pier's footing took years to resolve, but the most thrilling part of construction for locals was the placing of the first of the two great tubular trusses on their piers. The trusses were built on the river bank and would be placed on the base of the piers; they would then be raised by hydraulic presses as the masonry was built up beneath them.

Church bells were rung and flags hung from every house in Saltash as the locally declared holiday of 1 September 1857 dawned brilliantly clear. There was not a vantage point to be had as Brunel orchestrated, with coloured flags and large numbers on placards, the move of the tubes away from the river bank. They were mounted on pontoons and manoeuvred into place using the tide and adjustment of water in the pontoons to float and lower them. Brunel had asked for complete silence during the operation, and at the moment he took up his position on a platform on the tube, like a conductor, silence fell.

When the tube was in place, a great cheer rang out and a band of the Royal Marines played Handel's 'See, the conqu'ring hero comes'. But when Prince Albert came to open the bridge on 3 May 1859, Brunel was not present; his health had been broken by anxiety over his third ship, the gargantuan *Great Eastern*. Brunel's last sight of his great bridge was from a specially contrived wagon, which was drawn slowly across it by one of Gooch's locomotives, shortly before his death on 15 September.

Once in Cornwall, the glorious landscapes are enhanced by the frequent grandstand views afforded by the 34 viaducts between Plymouth and Truro. Trains pause at Liskeard, where the branch train to Looe waits in a platform at right angles to the main-line platforms before pirouetting down to the reversing point at Coombe Junction.

At Bodmin Parkway one may see a steam train of the Bodmin & Wenford Railway waiting to make a noisy exit up the hill to Bodmin General. After Par, the train climbs past the almost perfectly circular, dark stone shell keep of Restormel Castle, built on a 12th-century motte raised by the wonderfully named Baldwin FitzTurstin. St Austell became a world centre of china clay from the early 19th century and still is, as the white 'Cornish Alps' of waste to the north of the line attest.

From the viaduct at Truro the Gothic Revival cathedral, completed in 1910, can be admired at close quarters. There is little evidence around Redruth that it was once a major centre for tin and copper mining with smelting works, but the town had been at the forefront of industrial development. It was home to William Murdoch, who built a prototype steam locomotive before he moved to Birmingham and forged a partnership with James Watt, and his Redruth house was the first domestic residence to be lit by gas.

Palm trees lend an exotic air to St Erth, junction for the enchanting branch line to St Ives. The journey's *denouement* is provided by the dramatic outline of St Michael's Mount and its castle rising out of the sea as the train curves into the station at Penzance, memorably captured in paint by Stanhope Alexander Forbes, one of the founder members of the Newlyn School of Art.

How long: 3 hours

BELMOND'S TRAINS (SOUTHERN ENGLAND)

The company begun by James Sherwood to re-create the Orient Express (see page 101) operates three other trains in Britain, and no book of the world's great railway journeys could omit them, even though they operate varied itineraries. The British Pullman began operation in 1982 with a rake of sumptuous and exquisitely restored carriages dating from 1925. Previous users included the royal family, President de Gaulle and Nikita Khrushchev. It takes guests on the first stage of an Orient Express journey, from London to Folkestone, as well as day and weekend excursions in southern England.

The Northern Belle took to the rails in 2000 and, in the way its modern air-conditioned carriages have been rebuilt, evokes the 1930s 'Belle' trains that operated scenic excursions around northern England and Scotland. Both trains have departures from over 60 stations to a wide range of sporting and cultural events, country houses, castles and gardens, usually reached by connecting coaches. Sometimes a steam locomotive hauls the train. Lunch or dinner of four or five courses is served in exemplary style on starched

Photo: Craig Wallace

white linen in wood-panelled surroundings with deeply upholstered armchairs topped with antimacassars.

The third train is the Royal Scotsman, which tours the country on scenic and themed journeys, occasionally venturing south of the border. Belmond has refined the art of designing small but perfectly formed cabins decorated with marquetry panelling, all amenities and a surprisingly powerful shower in the en-suite bathroom. Dinners of remarkable sophistication are created in the galley kitchen and served in the two dining-cars at tables of four and six. Cheese and bannocks are served in the observation car during the varied post-prandial entertainment of Scottish traditional music and stories of Highland history.

A similar train for Ireland, the Grand Hibernian, starts operation in 2016.

How long: Mostly 8 hours–8 days

EUROSTAR (LONDON–PARIS)

No one could pretend the scenery between London and Paris or Brussels is going to inspire a modern-day Edward Thomas or John Betjeman, but the pleasure of using the magnificently restored station at St Pancras, the Channel Tunnel and the blissful ease of Eurostar makes it a great experience. Construction of the Channel Tunnel was not only an engineering triumph, but also testimony to the tenacity and skill of Sir Alastair Morton in keeping the many banks funding it on side. Hopefully a comparison between Eurostar and the aggravations of flying between the three capitals will also lead many to question why governments remain in thrall to short-haul aviation, despite the mounting environmental costs.

If any station encapsulates the romance of the railway, it is St Pancras. As Sir John Summerson said, 'no other structure in the world [captures] the moment of supreme optimism in the marriage of steam and progress'. Had the 1960s philistines at British Railways Board achieved their aim, St Pancras would have gone the way of Philip Hardwick's Doric Propylaeum at nearby Euston. Thanks to a campaign led by John Betjeman and the Victorian Society, wiser counsels prevailed and St Pancras was saved to become today's gateway to the Continent.

The Midland Grand Hotel, now St Pancras Chambers, and the train shed roof were both imposing architectural statements and innovative. George Gilbert Scott recycled some elements from a rejected Gothic design for the Foreign and Colonial offices in Whitehall to create London's most magnificent hotel when it opened in 1873. It used hydraulic power for its 'ascending rooms' (lifts) and was one of the first to have electric bells. There may have been a liberal supply of flushing lavatories, but the five floors of bedrooms had to share just nine bathrooms; a portable hip-bath added a shilling to the bill.

Its solidity and limited facilities for ablutions proved a severe handicap as rivals installed private bathrooms. The chairman of the London Midland & Scottish Railway Sir Josiah (later Lord) Stamp pointed out, 'It is impossible to put in a new piece of heating apparatus or anything of that kind without meeting the same obstacles that would be encountered in modifying the Rock of Gibraltar'. Such difficulties encouraged its conversion to offices after the hotel closed in 1935.

Photo: Florian Pépellin

In contrast, William Barlow's train shed has remained the perfect umbrella for passengers since 1868, its 25 soaring wrought-iron ribs forming what remained for almost a century the largest station roof in the world without internal support. They were made by Derbyshire's Butterley Company, whose ironwork can be seen in stations as far afield as Buenos Aires and which, by 1863, was rolling the largest masses of iron in the country. The train deck is still supported by many of the original 688 cast-iron columns, separated by dimensions determined by a barrel of Burton ale as well as structural requirements.

Leaving St Pancras, the Eurostar flashes through the white elephant of Stratford International and pauses in the bunker of Ebbsfleet station before the hash of clogged roads, wasteland and dismal sheds that forms much of north Kent beside the line. The crossing of the River Medway near Rochester provides the first uplifting view, and the traverse of the 'Garden of England' and its orchards is pleasant enough.

After the longueurs of the tunnel, the hurtle across Nord-Pas-de-Calais and Picardy, with their tree-lined canals and rivers interrupting the sweep of ploughed fields and hilltop woodland, is also pleasant. Though this is train travel where the pleasures of the destinations far exceed the 'getting there', it is for a still relatively new paradigm of inter-city travel that Eurostar earns a place.

How long: Paris 2 hours 15 minutes; Brussels 2 hours

MAINLAND EUROPE

BERGEN–OSLO (NORWAY)

Paradise or Hell is a choice for passengers in Norway; you can enter Hell near Trondheim and Paradis is a station on Bergen's light rail system that opened in 2010. Bergen's reputation for rain and overcast skies isn't what you would associate with paradise, but on a fine day the city's painted wooden houses along the waterfront at Bryggen are as fine a sight as you would expect for a World Heritage Site.

From 2016 the light rail line will link the airport with the city's fine railway station, opened in 1913 and built out of dark stone in the National Romantic style. Beyond it is a classic train shed sheltering the platforms from which trains leave for the capital, Oslo. It took 12 years to build this 489-kilometre (304-mile) railway, which was no mean feat given the difficulties: twelve different routes were surveyed before one was chosen; there were few roads for supplies; the severity of the winters allowed construction for just three or four months a year; and 18 kilometres (11.2 miles) of tunnel had to be bored, mostly through solid gneiss. Snow shelters had to be built to protect the most vulnerable sections of line, and one of the trains opening the first section in 1883 became embedded in snow. Small wonder that the area around Finse was chosen as the setting for Ice Planet Hoth in the 1980 film *The Empire Strikes Back*.

Leaving Bergen the train dives into the Ulriken Tunnel and soon reaches a cliff ledge overlooking a fjord with conifers clinging to the crags above the train. Reaching sea

Photo: Alasdair McLellan

level, the railway runs along a foreshore with boat houses dipping into the clear water. Occasional headlands are occupied by birch-sheltered wooden cabins painted in the distinctive dark ox-blood common to much of Norway.

After a long tunnel following Dale station, the railway runs beside the River Vossa, periodically crossed by attractive pedestrian suspension bridges, and descends to skirt a large lake. Voss station is the end of the commuter services from Bergen and was the place chosen for King Haakon VII to give a speech at the formal opening of the full railway in 1909, when he described the line as 'the greatest feat of our generation'.

After a brief stretch of upland farming country, the landscape becomes progressively wilder and the trees thin to hardy birch and pines. The train picks its way along a ledge high above the River Raundal as it flows through a spectacular canyon before reaching Mjølfjell station and a scattering of holiday cabins. A traveller in April 1910 recorded snow 3.6–4.6 metres (9.8–13.1 feet) deep at Upsete station through which a slit had been cut for the train, and tunnels had been burrowed through the snow to the first-floor windows to provide access to the booking office.

The climb towards the central plateau steepens and the last trees are left behind; it will be another 96 kilometres (60 miles) before another is seen. At the junction station of Myrdal, isolated in a great bowl of mountains, many break the journey for the spectacular branch down to the sea at Flåm, so steep that some trains built for the line had five braking systems. Myrdal station oscillates between utter quiet and manic activity as passengers from a cruise ship reach the summit of the climb from Flåm and flock into the large café and gift shop.

Leaving Myrdal there are glimpses down a precipice

over 600 metres (2,000 feet) deep down to Flåmsdal and Sognefjord. The line is soon twisting between mountains, and that strange phenomenon of being unable to tell where snow ends and sky begins is a common and disorienting experience. Only where a mountain face is too sheer for snow to adhere is there any colour in the landscape. Teams of straining huskies may be spotted carving a trail as the summit of the line is reached at Taugevann, at 1,303 metres (4,275 feet).

The course of the railway is surprisingly straight across the plateau, enabling a turn of speed that whips up the snow into eddying wraiths. The Hardangervidda is the largest mountain plateau in Europe, and there are few places as bleak and remote on a European railway as road-less Finse, the highest station on Norway's railways, at 1,222 metres (4,009 feet). The men on Scott's fateful 1912 expedition trained here, as did Shackleton's two years later, and it is a popular destination for cross-country skiing. Near the station is a museum about the navvies who built the railway, and there is a single, lonely hotel with its own bakery.

The handsome wooden station building at Haugastøl, in a cross between the National Romantic and Jugendstil styles, is the start of hiking routes through the shallow valleys of the high plateau and the beginning of the Rallar Road, which takes its name from the navvies who used it during construction of the railway. Today the track is regarded as a historic monument, ideal for mountain bikers; some even take advantage of the altitude to freewheel/cycle all the way to the sea at Bergen.

Holiday cabins dot the hills as the train heads for the north shore of Lake Ustevatn, which can be frozen for three-quarters of the year. A great valley with a frozen lake opens up to the right on the approach to Norway's best-known winter sports centre, Geilo, which boasts 32 downhill slopes and 220 kilometres (137 miles) of cross-country trails.

The train descends through the beautiful Hallingdal Valley, the frequent crossings of the river marked by a metallic roar. Past Ål, there is a dramatic stretch above the forested Hallingdalselva River, before reaching Flå and a shelf of rock high above Lake Krøderen. Farms return to the landscape before the junction of Hønefoss and the end of the Bergen line.

The final stretch through Drammen runs beside the large lake of Tyrifjorden and then the sea, with views over the Dramsfjord and its islands, before a long tunnel under the city delivers the train into Oslo S (Oslo Central).

How long: 7 hours

THE HARZ MOUNTAINS (GERMANY)

The Harz Mountains of Saxony-Anhalt were first given a wide audience by Goethe, who climbed its highest point, the Brocken, in 1777 and chose it as the setting for the scene in his play, *Faust*, when witches indulge in revelry on Walpurgis Night (30 April). The mountains were the subject of Heinrich Heine's travelogue *The Harz Journey* in 1826, and the Brocken's mystique was enlarged by the curious spectral effects caused by giant shadows of visitors on mist or cloud.

The narrow-gauge railway that opened to the summit in 1899 is part of a 140-kilometre (87-mile) network of lines linking the enchanting towns and villages of the area, renowned for their timber-framed houses – Quedlinburg is a World Heritage Site for the 1,500 examples in the old town. The system carries over a million passengers a year, mostly tourists, though schoolchildren and shoppers also use the trains.

The steam trains of the Harzer Schmalspur Bahnen (HSB) provide probably the greatest daily steam spectacle of the Continent, with its huge gleaming black tank locomotives battling the steep gradients. The oldest date from 1897 and are known as Mallets, with two sets of cylinders, one articulated to help negotiate sharp radius curves. The youngest are colossal behemoths built as recently as 1956, which thunder up the steepest line to the Brocken and over the 'main line' between Wernigerode and Nordhausen.

The carriages have open-end balconies, and for many they are the best place to enjoy a journey. It affords the physical pleasure of inhaling fresh mountain air tinged with pine resin and the occasional whiff of steam and hot oil, coupled with the stentorian bark of the locomotive echoing from the forest that shrouds some sections.

Most visitors begin their journey at the three stations with connections to the Deutsche Bahn national network, at Wernigerode and Quedlinburg in the north and Nordhausen in the south. The character of the lines that make up the network is so different that it is well worth buying the three- or five-day tickets giving unlimited travel to allow time to explore the many fascinating places that can be reached by the trains.

Wernigerode is the largest station and the headquarters of the HSB, where the locomotive workshops and largest engine shed are located beside Westerntor station on the edge of the old town. The workshops maintain the seventeen regularly used steam locomotives built by Lokomotivbau Karl Marx in Babelsberg near Berlin and the eight historic locomotives

Photo: calflier001

used on special occasions. The lengthy trains on the main line to Nordhausen and on the branch to Brocken include bar and buffet cars and even open carriages in summer.

Trains leave Wernigerode by squeezing between the houses and weaving past gardens. With bell clanging for the level crossing near the 13th-century West Gate, they set off alongside the road before climbing steeply into the woods to reach the rural junction of Drei Annen Hohne. The station building has a good restaurant from which to watch three trains meet.

From here, most passengers head up the branch to the Brocken, an almost continuous climb at 1 in 30 through dense coniferous forest. The forest floor is a mass of moss-covered rocks, wind-blown trunks and pine cones. Suddenly the trees end and the train emerges into open grassland and an extraordinary panorama over nothing but trees. The train curls round the former Cold War listening post to the summit station.

From Drei Annen Hohne, southbound trains cross an undulating upland plateau of forest and meadow clearings, filled with wild flowers in spring. The summit is Benneckenstein, where the station building has a flat for rent and a small museum. The line drops down to the quiet wooded junction of Eisfelder Talmühle, which still retains the atmosphere of an East German narrow-gauge junction with its huge three-storey station building and reopened restaurant. Nordhausen trains continue to Ilfeld, where forest gives way to open country dotted with halts for Nordhausen students and shoppers. The line ends alongside the tram stop in the forecourt of Nordhausen station.

Far fewer visitors allow time for the line east from Eisfelder Talmühle, not realising what a different experience the line to Quedlinburg offers. A climb up the steep-sided valley of the River Behre brings the train to lonely Birkenmoor in a woodland clearing. From the junction of Stiege a line heads north to Hasselfelde, where an incongruous Wild West village known as Pullman City has shows illustrating the life of cowboys.

A willow-shaded river and grazing cattle keep the railway company on the way to the neatly laid-out former mining village of Strassberg and its prominent church tower. Yet another line wanders off at the junction of Alexisbad to the small town of Harzgerode, where trains terminate beside the 16th-century castle.

Many European countries had narrow-gauge railways serving remoter country areas, and it was a common practice to lay them beside unmetalled roads. Leaving Alexisbad, there is a remnant of this roadside arrangement running through Drahtzug to reach Mägdesprung, where the remains of an ironworks founded by Prince Frederick Albert of Anhalt can still be seen from the train. Whistling furiously for a level crossing, the locomotive roars up the steepest gradient on the line, skirting some artificial lakes and orchards on the approach to Gernrode.

It is well worth breaking the journey here to see the magnificent Romanesque church of St Cyriakus, built in 960–65, before continuing through an open, agricultural landscape to reach Quedlinburg. Besides an old town of cobbled streets full of wonderful vernacular buildings, the town has an imposing 16th-century castle and several fine churches – one with a double-storey look-out sentry box attached to a spire.

How long: journey times across the network vary

COLOGNE–FRANKFURT VIA KOBLENZ OR NEUWIED (GERMANY)

The Rhine south of Bonn is one of the most dramatic stretches of river in Europe, celebrated in verse, notably by Byron in *Childe Harold's Pilgrimage*, and in paint by Turner and countless artists. The Rhine was the subject of the first Baedecker guide book, published in 1834 in conjunction with John Murray.

Railway lines busy with passenger and freight trains run along both banks, and the hills rise so steeply above the railways that to see the string of castles along their ridges you have to travel along both routes, providing a quite different perspective on the river. It's a perfect day itinerary from Cologne, where the station is close to the immense French Gothic-style cathedral; begun in 1248, it wasn't even finished when Napoleon's troops used it as a stable, being finally completed in 1880.

Taking an early train south along the east bank should catch some sun on the west. The river is reached just south of Bonn, only a cycle path separating the railway from the water. Commuter housing gives way to orchards and terraced vines. Near the resort of Königswinter is one of only four rack railways in Germany, which since 1883 has been taking visitors up to Drachenfels, one of the wooded volcanic hills along the east bank known as the Siebengebirge. Passing Bad Hönningen, the castle of Rheineck can be seen above the village of Brohl on the west bank.

The approach to Koblenz is unmistakable. On the spit that marks the mouth of the Mosel stands the imposing equestrian statue of Emperor Wilhelm I, a replica of the original erected in 1897. Close by is the 13th-century headquarters of the Order of Teutonic Knights, now home to the Ludwig Museum, and the Romanesque 12th-century Basilica of St Castor. The railway passes underneath the cablecar recently built to take visitors up to the vast Ehrenbreitstein Fortress.

Soon after Niederlahnstein is the junction for another enchanting railway journey, along the Lahn Valley to Giessen. A great yellow edifice high on the west bank is Stolzenfels, where Queen Victoria stayed in 1845. One of the loveliest sections follows the wisteria-clad station at Osterspai, the river and railways on both banks describing tight loops, which pose a challenge for the longer barges. The river is busy with freight traffic at all times of the year and during summer with excursion vessels. At some point in the journey, most passengers enjoy the sight of the last paddlesteamer, the *Goethe* of 1913, though sadly her paddles are turned by diesel rather than steam engines.

The succession of castles continues, prominently the mid-river Pfalz built in the 11th century to collect river tolls. In the adjacent village of Kaub is a statue of Field-Marshall Blücher of Waterloo fame, marking the place where he crossed the Rhine in 1813. After the resort and wine centre of Rüdesheim, the railway parts company with the river and the vine-filled hills recede and reduce in height. At the historic spa town of Wiesbaden, state capital of Hesse, the train reverses to reach Frankfurt-am-Main, where half a day allows time to see Goethe's house and the pedestrianised main square, the Römerberg.

Returning by the west bank to Cologne, the train stops at the sandstone city of Mainz with its Gutenberg Museum and magnificent Romanesque cathedral, the interior at its most atmospheric in fading light late on a winter afternoon. In contrast to Cologne, it was built in just 12 years, between 997 and 1009.

Photo: Norbert Hüttisch, Karlsruhe

Just as the eye is tiring of acres of orchard and market gardens, the extraordinary plinthed statue of Germania comes into view on the opposite bank. Unveiled in 1883, it commemorates the unification of Germany in 1871 following the Franco-Prussian War.

For over a century, Bingen has been the place where passengers transferred between river steamer and train, but the town is best known for the remarkable polymath Abbess Hildegard of Bingen, who spent most of her 81 years in the nearby Benedictine monastery.

The necklace of castles continues on the opposite bank, but there are no vineyards until Boppard is reached because the hillsides are too steep. Behind the town walls of Bacharach is a jewel of a medieval village with streets of half-timbered houses. The bend in the river at Lorelei is made treacherous by the currents, but it is the towering basalt rock that has made it famous as far afield as the Bronx in New York, where there is a Lorelei Monument based on the legend inspired by the rock and the murmur it creates.

Boppard's position on the great loop in the river attracted the Romans, and remains of their camp can be seen between the railway and the river. A scenic branch line heads west from Boppard into the Hunsrück, the area made famous by Edgar Reisz's epic film series *Heimat*. The 15-kilometre (9.3-mile) line to Emmelshausen crosses the impressive Hubertus Viaduct and provides access to a cycle route along the now closed railway line beyond Emmelshausen.

After Spay, the impressive central tower of Marksburg Castle soars above the other buildings. It was the only Rhenish castle that withstood siege during the Thirty Years War and remains a fine medieval fortress. Less inspiring is the bulk of Lahneck Castle, defended according to legend by the last of the Knights Templar in 1312.

After Koblenz, the great square towers of the Catholic church in Andernach rise above the walled town. Another branch line, but one still steam worked on certain days, runs west from Brohl to Engeln. At Remagen the train passes the site of the famous bridge captured intact in March 1945, allowing five divisions to cross the Rhine into the Ruhr before it finally collapsed under repeated bombardment from land and air.

The last major stop before Cologne is the former West German capital of Bonn, where the Rheinisches Landesmuseum and the Romantic Rhine Art Gallery provide an excellent introduction to the area.

How long: 1 hour 30 minutes–3 hours 30 minutes

NÎMES–CLERMONT-FERRAND (FRANCE)

This is unquestionably one of France's finest journeys, though shamefully neglected and underpromoted by SNCF – like the parallel eastern route between Béziers and Clermont-Ferrand. Properly developed and managed, the two lines could form part of a fine scenic circuit.

The Ligne de Cévennes climbs into the desolate uplands of the eastern Massif Central and through the Cévennes to the Auvergne. The southern part between La Grand-Combe and Alès opened as early as 1839 to carry coal, using locomotives built in Newcastle-upon-Tyne. It was engineered by the man known as the 'French Stephenson', Paulin Talabot, who became a friend of Robert Stephenson and went on to build much of the rest of the line, which opened in nine stages to allow through running from March 1870.

Photo: Georges Seguin (Okki)

There is a strong sense of the Mediterranean about the city of departure and the landscapes of the early part of this journey. Nîmes is sometimes called the French Rome because of its arena (amphitheatre) for 24,000 spectators, nearby Pont du Gard aqueduct and the finely preserved example of a Roman temple, the Maison Carrée of AD 4–7.

The train extricates itself from the city through some deep limestone cuttings to reach a plain strewn with cypress, Lombardy poplars and Aleppo pines. By Fons-St-Mamert, the first vineyards appear, and for mile after mile, there is little to divert the eye from vines until Vézénobres, where there are fragmentary relics of the coal-mines that encouraged construction of the railway. Mines could once be found up the Gardon Valley as far as La Grand'Combe, and there was once enough freight traffic to warrant a hump shunting yard at Alès.

Louis Pasteur came to Alès to study diseases of the silkworm used in the town's silk trade. A little later, Robert Louis Stevenson ended his journey through the Cévennes here and boarded a train; his 12-day hike with the stubborn donkey Modestine culminated in the classic 1879 *Travels with a Donkey in the Cévennes*. Leaving the town, the gradient steepens as the climb into the Cévennes begins, often switching valleys through tunnels.

It is astonishing that a railway should have been built through such sparsely populated and difficult terrain, which required 106 tunnels and 1,300 viaducts and bridges in 300 kilometres (186 miles). The hillsides are so precipitous that many have had to be terraced to support agriculture. A great curve of masonry carries the railway above the small town of Chamborigaud on a viaduct of 39 arches, completed in 1867, with great views over the folds of purple hills that stretch to the horizon.

The high level of the railway continues to give panoramic views over the woods and the huggermugger houses of the little town of Villefort that fill a trench in the valley below. A water tower and cranes for steam locomotives still survive, half a century after the last whistle was heard. Emerging from a tunnel soon after Villefort, the train bursts out of the dark on to a viaduct across the Lac de Rachas reservoir. Through forests of pine and larch and along hillside ledges, the train climbs to the line's 1,023-metre (3,356-foot) summit at La Bastide-St Laurent-les-Bains, close to the source of the River Allier and the watershed that separates rivers flowing into the Atlantic and the Mediterranean.

Beginning a long companionship with the waters of the Allier, the railway reaches Langogne, its Romanesque church protectively encircled by houses and five rampart towers. As though the scenery had not been captivating enough, the line delivers its *pièce de résistance* with a series of stunning views along the gorges and narrow valley of the Allier as the river alternately rushes and glides towards the north. Occasionally huge rocks from the heights frustrate the flow, explaining the need for the avalanche wires above the railway to alert neighbouring stations of danger.

Passengers enjoy a grandstand view of this beauty, since the train runs almost continuously on a shelf created by retaining walls directly above the water, only deviating from the river where it describes a meander and the train burrows into a tunnel through a promontory. Past Alleyras there is another gorge so narrow and deep that in winter the sun hardly penetrates the bottom, where ancient wizened trees are appropriately covered in old man's beard.

After this spectacular section, the train parts company with the Allier as the valley flattens into a landscape of orchards and pasture. On a hillside bluff stands the huge fortified abbey church of Chanteuges. After Langeac there is a final climb to reach a plateau of bracken-covered heath, followed by farms fringed with lines of trees as windbreaks.

The market town of Brioude boasts the finest Romanesque abbey church in the Auvergne; the basilica of St Julien was built in the early 13th century on the site of the martyr's decapitation.

Digital platform indicators at Arvant herald the approach to Clermont-Ferrand, though there is a final flourish with the sight of the volcanic plugs for which the area is famous. Even the city's double-spired cathedral was built out of black volcanic rock, though the city is probably best known for its links with road rather than rail transport – it is home to the Michelin man, Bibendum.

How long: 5 hours

THROUGH THE DRAC GORGE TO LA MURE (FRANCE)

France was once laced with an extraordinary number of characterful narrow-gauge railways. Few remain, but one of the most dramatically situated survivors is the Chemin de Fer de La Mure (CFLM) in the Isère south of Grenoble. The metre-gauge (3 feet 3 inches) line runs for 30 kilometres (18.6 miles) from St Georges de Commiers on the SNCF Grenoble–Veynes–Briançon line to the former coal-mining area of La Mure: coal was the reason for the line's construction.

Unusually the railway was electrified as early as 1903, and electric locomotives of 1932 vintage still haul trains over what is now a heritage railway operation, augmented by rolling

Photo: Jvillafruela

stock from Swiss lines. The CFLM has not had an easy time of it; the steep-sided mountains are prone to landslides, and in 2010 a huge landslide closed the line. It is hoped that a new operator will reintroduce a service over part of the line from 2016, but it is advisable to check the situation before visiting.

It is best to sit on the right. The journey wends up a wooded valley through hay meadows and walnut orchards to reach the deep gorge of the River Drac beyond Notre Dame. The line clings to the almost sheer face, sometimes on arched viaducts built against the rock, with progressively wider views over the ranges of the Vercors massif. Wide-eaved Alpine houses with tell-tale wood piles stacked up below them make up the hamlets as the line twists and turns to gain height. Two parallel viaducts over the Loulla chasm are at different levels, reflecting the rate of climb and linked by a horseshoe curve.

The line's summit is in the tunnel under the Col de la Festinière, which brings the train into a wide valley (frequented by skiers in winter) that still retains vestiges of the coal-mining that once sustained its population. La Mure has plenty of good restaurants and, in the station building, a museum about the history of this remarkable railway.

How long: line yet to reopen

TO ISTANBUL BY ORIENT EXPRESS (FRANCE–TURKEY)

The name Georges Nagelmackers probably means nothing to most Belgians today, yet this entrepreneur from Liège created a train whose name is famous throughout the world. The first run of the Orient Express took place on 4 October

1883, when a train of five carriages – two *fourgons* or luggage vans, a dining-car and two sleeping-car saloons – left Gare du Strasbourg (now Gare de l'Est) in the evening.

On board were two dozen guests, invited by Nagelmackers in the hope that their connections or newspaper reports would encourage others to patronise this radical new approach to international travel. Though they were to be cocooned in unprecedented comfort, some carried revolvers in case of mischief in the brigand-infested Balkans. This was no empty fear; in May 1891 the Orient Express was derailed and robbed by bandits less than 100 kilometres (62 miles) from Istanbul.

The guests were astounded by their accommodation. Their compartments were walled in marquetry panels of mahogany and teak, and two red plush armchairs for day use gave way to generously upholstered beds with silk sheets, the upper berth folded down from the wall. The gas-lit dining-car was opulently decorated and served food and wines appropriate to the country being passed through. It was the beginning of luxury train travel in Europe and the birth of a legendary name.

Its history since has filled books and innumerable articles, some confused by the fact that between 25 May 1982 and 12 December 2009 there were two trains that could claim to be the Orient Express: on the earlier date, the Venice Simplon-Orient-Express was inaugurated by James Sherwood, launching the train that has become a byword for luxury train travel today; and on the later date EuroNight train number 469 'Orient Express' left Strasbourg for Vienna for the last time. With this departure, the famous name disappeared from the timetable of scheduled service trains.

It was hardly mourned, since it had become a shadow of Nagelmackers' Compagnie Internationale des Wagons-

Lits (CIWL) trains, and their lustre has been brilliantly recaptured by the Venice Simplon-Orient-Express. Composed of magnificently restored carriages dating from 1926 to 1931, the train operates a frequent service between Paris and Venice, but the pearl is the annual re-run of the 1883 route to Istanbul.

Departure from Gare de l'Est is still an occasion: a band plays as passengers walk the red carpet to their royal blue carriages. Paris commuters look on with understandable envy as the train glides through the unlovely suburbs, so nothing is lost by spending the first hour exploring one's compartment and the history of the carriage. During the Second World War, CIWL carriages were scattered to the four winds and some ended up in ignominious or dubious roles. You might find you are travelling in a coach that had served as a hotel in Lyons, or a brothel in Limoges.

Convivial pre-prandials are served in the bar car as the railway follows the course of the Canal de la Marne. The sound of a grand piano fills the art nouveau-decorated car, and most people are dressed in appropriately elegant attire.

Dinner is served while passing through Haute-Saône and for the first night the carriages claim more attention than the landscapes passing by, though the Maitre d'hôtel tries to ring the changes each night so that everyone can appreciate the decorative differences between the three dining-cars: the marquetry flower baskets of the 'Etoile du Nord'; the René Lalique-designed Bacchanalian maidens of 'Côte d'Azur'; and the black lacquer panels of chinoiserie in 'L'Oriental', depicting sporting animals. Polished crystal and silver gleam in the warm lights of the dining cars as people settle into the generous armchairs.

The challenge of producing 100 elaborate dinners in the confines of two narrow galley kitchens on a moving train would defeat most head chefs, but not Executive Head Chef Christian Bodiguel. In 2014 he celebrated 30 years with the Orient Express, giving guests a gastronomic experience with such dishes as seabass in a coat of thinly sliced potatoes with sevruga caviar, dill and sour cream, followed by roast best end of lamb coated in mustard seeds.

The train traverses the alpine delights of Switzerland, Liechtenstein and western Austria during the night, necessitated by the constraints of railway timetables and the train's overnight stops in Budapest and Bucharest. Dawn is breaking as the train nears Salzburg, and the last snow-dusted crags are still in sight before the lower peaks of the Salzkammergut begin to line the southern horizon. A mercifully light breakfast of rolls and croissants with a thermos of coffee is brought to your compartment as the train bowls across fertile farmland.

To the north of the line near Melk is the forbidding Benedictine monastery that was used in the filming of Umberto Eco's dark novel *The Name of the Rose*, with Sean Connery playing a medieval Hercule Poirot. Agatha Christie herself was as familiar with the Orient Express as her thriller set on the train would suggest; she regularly used it on her way to the Middle East and the archaeological excavations conducted by her husband. The marooning of the train by snow happened in February 1929, when it was snowbound for ten days in western Turkey.

Lunch comes at a good moment, for the flat landscapes on the western approaches to Vienna give a hint of the Little Hungarian Plain to come. Skirting Vienna, the train makes for the border, pausing at the first station on Hungarian soil, Hegyeshalom. Before the fall of the Iron Curtain, this border crossing was like a scene out of a John le Carré novel: the train was held in the open away from any

Photo: Kabelleger / David Gubler

platform, with watchtowers at each corner of the train and a soldier with a German Shepherd dog beside each door. Panels were unscrewed in the hope of finding contraband, while passports and belongings were scrutinised with dour suspicion. Today it is all smiles and courtesy.

There is no mistaking the Little Hungarian Plain that begins around Gyor: fields of cereals as far as the eye can see are broken up by willow-lined watercourses or stands of poplars acting as wind-breaks. Arrival at Budapest, the first overnight stop, is heralded by the bridge over a gentle curve on the Danube and a splendid view to the north of the historic buildings on Castle Hill. A uniformed band plays passengers into the former royal waiting room at Nyugati station, while press and television cameras record the annual arrival of a train that draws enough onlookers to warrant rope barriers. Much of the splendid iron framework of Nyugati station was cast in Paris for Eiffel, whose company built the station in 1874–7.

'I have never enjoyed a city more', wrote Jan Morris when she returned from a post-communist Christmas in Budapest. It is a spectacular city, best appreciated from Castle Hill in Buda and the white stone walls of Fishermen's Bastion, looking out over the sweep of the Danube to Pest, fronted by the immense neo-Gothic Parliament building. Castle Hill itself is a lozenge-shaped enclave bounded by some of the city's most attractive residential streets to the north and the former royal palace in the south. In the centre is the 13th-century Matthias church, which became the city's main mosque for the 145 years of Turkish occupation from 1541, until liberated by a pan-European army.

After a two-hour private boat trip along the Danube, which is not blue, the train continues east across the Great Hungarian Plain. Prairie-sized fields of maize are interrupted by villages with trim plots of vegetables and the occasional lake surrounded by small dachas, bolt-holes from the city for the more affluent. Night masks the transition into Romania and with it a step back in time to strip fields and densely nucleated villages with trellised vines growing between the cottages.

At Braşov, the forested climb into the Carpathian Mountains begins, and their 'pearl' is Sinaia, where another band greets passengers before the coach transfer to the summer residence built in 1873–83 for King Carol I. Peleş Castle has a historic connection with the Orient Express, for the king extended an invitation to the guests aboard the first train to visit his newly built palace. The heavy decoration of the 116-room castle, its walls covered with ceremonial weapons, is unchanged today, as thankfully is the glorious mountain setting.

The Athénée Palace Hilton Hotel is an appropriate choice for the second night off the train because it has regained the elegance that attracted to its famous English Bar the central characters in Olivia Manning's *Balkan Trilogy*. There the impoverished Russian émigré Prince Yakimov meets journalists and other exiled aristocrats as well as Guy and Harriet Pringle, who were played by Kenneth Branagh and Emma Thompson in the BBC adaptation for television. A dinner of regional dishes is accompanied by a Romanian band playing the exuberant folk and gypsy music that inspired Romania's greatest composer, Georges Enescu.

Crossing the immense bridge over the Danube on the border between Romania and Bulgaria, the Orient Express turns south east through what was wild country in 1883, where bandits periodically raided stations. Much of it is still desolate, and unusually the railway follows a ridge for many miles, affording broad views over gently rolling grassland

and woods on both sides with the occasional town nestling in a depression.

At the Black Sea resort of Varna, coaches take guests to another building with an Orient Express connection: the 1880s summer villa of the Bulgarian Tsars incorporates the tympanum of a French château, which was cut into pieces and transported from Paris to Varna by the Orient Express.

Next morning the Turkish border formalities are whiled away by a display of national dances. Few railway approaches to the world's great cities can rival Istanbul, as the train descends to run along the Sea of Marmara with the gap-tooth remnants of the great walls recalling the ancient ebb and flow of Christendom and Islam. The train curves round under the walls of the Topkapi Palace to another musical welcome at Sirkeci terminus and a reluctant acceptance of journey's end. Glasses of Turkish tea are served in the tall-ceilinged former royal waiting room while transfers to hotels are organised and luggage unloaded.

Istanbul is not a city to be rushed. Whether admiring Justinian's underground reservoir of AD 532, with its 336 marble columns, the Blue Mosque, Santa Sophia, the Topkapi Palace and the 16th-century Süleymaniye Mosque, which inspired a pastiche in London's Kew Gardens two centuries later, or watching the shipping on the Golden Horn, it is a city that should be savoured at leisure.

For Orient Express passengers, the Pera Palace is the obvious choice of hotel. Opened by the CIWL in 1892, it remained Istanbul's only luxury hotel for decades. The room where Agatha Christie wrote *Murder on the Orient Express* is preserved, but the wonderful brass plates on bedroom doors naming previous occupants were swept away in an insensitive restoration. They included Mata Hari, Josephine

Baker, Greta Garbo, Ernest Hemingway, Edward VIII and Leon Trotsky.

How long: 2–6 days

TO THE ROOF OF EUROPE (SWITZERLAND)

If those on whirlwind European tours do only one thing in Switzerland, it's likely to be the journey from Interlaken up to Jungfraujoch, Europe's highest railway station, at 3,454 metres (11,332 feet). The scenery is spellbinding, as is the panorama down Europe's longest glacier from the mountain's restaurants and viewing platforms.

From Interlaken, the train races across flat ground to dive into the narrow defile of the Lütschine river to reach the junction of Wilderswil, where those with time can take the cogwheel train to Schynige Platte and stupendous views over the lakes of Thun and Brienz. At Zweilütschinen the train divides, usually the rear section turning east to Grindelwald while those heading for Jungfraujoch continue south in the front section to Lauterbrunnen. The valley walls are so steep and tall that sunlight hardly reaches some parts, and there is little room for more than the railway, the White Lütschine and the road between the vertiginous forested flanks.

In a rare instance for Switzerland of poor planning, the section between Lauterbrunnen and Kleine Scheidegg was built to a different gauge from the railways at each end, necessitating an easy change of train at both places. Leaving Lauterbrunnen, the railway twists its way up to the sunny slope on which the car-free resort of Wengen is laid out,

Photo: Maksym Kozlenko

with a glorious view along the Lauterbrunnen valley with its 72 waterfalls. The railway heaves itself up to the saddle of rock on which Kleine Scheidegg sits, every curve of the line opening up a new panorama over the mountains.

Kleine Scheidegg is a good place to break the journey and catch a later train, perhaps having a hot chocolate on the terrace to take in the stupendous sight of the Eiger, Mönch and Jungfrau. A short section of railway brings you to Eigergletscher station, where for many years Greenland Dogs giving sledge rides at the summit were kennelled; they were descended from six Greenland Dogs imported in 1913 with the help of the polar explorer Roald Amundsen. Just beyond is the portal to the 7-kilometre (4.3-mile) tunnel, much of it through unlined rock, which terminates inside the Jungfrau.

For over a decade, Swiss engineers tried to devise a way to make the spectacle from the mountain available to all for the price of a train ticket. The 'Eureka' moment came when Adolf Guyer-Zeller was walking with his daughter on the Schilthorn in August 1893. He suddenly realised that the way to build it was a tunnel from the railhead at Kleine Scheidegg rather than through the White Lütschine valley from Lauterbrunnen. He stayed up much of the night in his Mürren hotel room, sketching out the ideas that would be followed almost to the letter.

The plan was to build an open section of railway to the start of tunnelling beyond a station at Eigergletscher; once tunnelling began, work could be progressed round the clock and all year using electrically powered drills on the hard rock. The railway would then be opened in stages to generate revenue: short foot tunnels from two stations inside the rock would allow passengers to visit viewing windows over the valleys from the wall of the mountain. Ascending trains still stop at the cavernous stations of Eigerwand (Eiger Wall) and Eismeer for passengers to enjoy the panoramas.

Even water for the workers was a problem since the sources froze with the onset of winter, so engineers came up with a clever electrical device capable of melting large quantities of snow. The bitter cold and the difficulty of getting supplies to the workings necessitated a huge stockpile of food and equipment being created at Eigergletscher during the summer months. The most spectacular disaster occurred in 1908, when 30 tonnes of dynamite exploded near Eiger Wall, shattering windows in Grindelwald and creating a noise that was said to have been heard in Germany. Guyer-Zeller never lived to see the tunnel and railway finally opened in 1912, after 16 years' work.

From the unlined rock cavern where trains terminate, lifts take passengers to different levels serving the various facilities that have been created on the mountain, such as the Sphinx Observatory, which has a glazed observation hall to give views in all directions and down the gently curving 22-kilometre (13.7-mile) Aletsch glacier, one of the greatest sights in Europe.

How long: 2 hours 15 minutes

THE GLACIER EXPRESS (SWITZERLAND)

One of Europe's longest-running named trains is something of a misnomer: it was never an express unless limited stops justify the word and the glacier after which it was named has been done for by climate change. But for many, it is Europe's finest train journey, with barely a dull moment and an astonishing variety of mountain landscapes during its 290 kilometres (180 miles).

Since 1930 the train has linked the famous Swiss resorts of Zermatt and St Moritz, and it's always had special carriages, none more impressive than today's panoramic coaches that allow everyone to enjoy gazing up at the peaks without getting a cricked neck. A headphone commentary available in umpteen languages tells you what you're looking at, and in first class a meal is served at your seat. Running over the narrow-gauge tracks of the Matterhorn Gotthard Bahn and the Rhätische Bahn, the train averages just 36 km/h (22.4 mph) as it loops and spirals up and down the mountains of the Valais and Graubünden.

Until 1865, Zermatt was a little-known mountain farming village at the end of a track up the Matter Valley. Tragedy put it on the world stage when Edward Whymper conquered the Matterhorn but four of his party fell to their deaths on the descent. By the end of the decade the two main hotels had tripled their number of beds, but it was the arrival of the railway in 1891 that made it one of Switzerland's most popular mountain resorts. For some, it is a revelation how pleasant a town without cars can be – only a few electric vehicles whisper through Zermatt's narrow streets carrying luggage from the railway station.

With the precision for which Swiss railways and much else in the country are noted, the train doors hiss closed as the hand counting the seconds reaches the minute of departure. The train is soon running alongside the Matter Vispa River and describing a wide curve around a monumental jumble of boulders and scree covering two-thirds of the narrow valley floor. This was the result of the side of a mountain collapsing into the valley in 1991.

Stone covers the roofs of many chalets, their woodwork weathered to the colour of dark chocolate and the perfect foil for the bright red geraniums filling window and balcony boxes. Waterfalls, barns on staddle-stones and an onion-domed neo-Romanesque church at St Niklaus catch the eye before the train drops down a rack section into the Rhone Valley. Cogwheels underneath the train engage a rack between the rails, helping the locomotive to claw its way uphill and retard the descents. Inevitably, it was the Swiss who developed the US-invented concept, helping to expand tourism and winter sports in areas previously inaccessible to all but climbers.

Visp and Brig are major railway junctions and mark the eastern end of the industrialised part of the Rhone Valley, giving way to steep mountainsides all the way to what's left of its glacier. Cablecars from valley-floor stations rise to ski and hiking resorts so high above the river that they are often out of sight. After Morel railway, river and road squeeze through a narrow gorge before reaching the first spiral of the journey. After crossing Grengiols Viaduct, the highest bridge on the line at 91 metres (299 feet), the line curves sharply left inside a tunnel to loop round over itself and emerge high above the lower level.

Climbing through forests of pine, spruce and birch, the train reaches the upper Goms. The train races along the broad valley through a succession of densely nucleated villages composed of chalets and wizened barns on staddle stones. It was from Niederwald that César Ritz set out on his travels around the world from which he developed ideas for the hotels that would make him 'the hotelier of kings and king of hoteliers'. By a strange coincidence, the next village, Blitzingen, was home to the Seiler family, who created the best hotels in Zermatt.

Photo: Daniel Schwen

Ahead, mountains crowned with snow signal the approach to the Furka Pass, which links the Valais and canton Uri. Until 1982, the Glacier Express swung north at Oberwald to climb steeply towards the Furka Tunnel, with fine views over the Rhone glacier, before dropping down to Realp. Winter conditions were so severe, particularly on the east side of the tunnel, that the line could not be operated in winter; one bridge was so susceptible to avalanches that a collapsible bridge was designed, enabling it to be taken away in October and re-erected at the end of May.

The inability to run trains for eight months of the year prompted construction of the 15-kilometre (9.3-mile) Furka base tunnel, allowing year-round operation from 1982 and closure of the costly section between Oberwald and Realp. However, the line between Realp and Gletsch has been reopened by preservationists using Swiss-built rack steam locomotives, some repatriated from Vietnam where they survived the war, locked away in a shed hidden by jungle.

During the stop at Andermatt, passengers can look east to the mountain, which the railway climbs like a hairpin mountain road in a series of U-shaped loops. Lunch is served after departure, and once at the top of the climb, Andermatt looks Lilliputian. With a final twist, the train turns into the long valley of the Vorderrhein and the wildest section of the journey. The desolate valley has the feel and look of a Scottish glen, with rock outcrops piercing the tussock grass and gorse, and eagles riding the thermals. Near the 2,033-metre (6,670-foot) summit of the railway at Oberalppasshöhe, the infant Rhine is so narrow that you can jump across it.

At Disentis the train passes the vast white-walled Benedictine monastery of St Martin, thought to have been founded by an Irish monk named Sigisbert in about 700. Alcohol, though not Benedictine, may be on passengers' minds at this point as the maître d' does his party trick of pouring grappa from a height into small glasses after lunch is over.

One of the highlights of the journey is the Rhine gorge east of Ilanz, known as Switzerland's 'Grand Canyon'. The tree-fringed limestone cliffs above the river are peppered with bizarre pinnacles and contorted shapes, making it a popular place for white-water rafting and canoeing. Shortly before Reichenau-Tamins, the railway crosses the Vorderrhein near its confluence with the Hinterrhein, the waters becoming the Rhine and flowing north to reach the North Sea in the Netherlands.

Having reversed at Chur, the train heads south beside the Hinterrhein to reach the valley of the Albula and the tunnel that will take the railway under the Albula Pass. From Thusis, the railway has been designated one of the world's three railway World Heritage Sites because of the extraordinary feat of engineering in lifting the line to the summit tunnel, but also the way the railway has blended with and complemented its beautiful natural setting.

Shortly before Filisur is Switzerland's most famous railway viaduct, frequently used in posters and books: the Landwasser Viaduct is famous for its graceful curve and the way the final arch springs from a sheer wall of rock where the line enters a tunnel.

Beyond Filisur, the engineers contrived an ingenious series of three horseshoe loops and three spirals, often in tunnel, to avoid the need for rack assistance, raising the line a vertical height of 416 metres (1,365 feet) in 13 kilometres (8 miles). Even with a map, passengers are bewildered by the twists and turns and one can understand why some doubted the confidence of the builders. No other railway in the world can rival this concentration of viaducts, corkscrews and curlicues.

In a former armoury and military store at Bergün, a

museum about the railway has been created with one of the old 'Crocodile' electric locomotives that operated over the line. Bergün is also the end of the 12.6-kilometre (7.8-mile) toboggan run from the summit station of Preda along a closed road, which is even lit by hurricane lamps at night. Toboggans can be hired at Preda station, and a train shuttle from Bergün returns passengers and toboggans to Preda until late in the evening.

A new summit tunnel is being built to replace the 5.8-kilometre (3.6-mile) bore opened in 1904, which was through such difficult rock that it took five years to construct. From the tunnel, the train descends through the delightful, sparsely populated valley of the River Bever to Samedan and the meeting point of three valleys and a triangle of lines, with Pontresina at the southern apex. Passing the foot of the Cresta Run at Celerina, the train climbs through spruce and larch into St Moritz, summer and winter sports capital of the Engadine.

Given the resort's status today as being 'more Bulgari than Burton', as someone put it, it's extraordinary that its first winter visitors, from Britain, had to be bribed to stay. The hotelier Johannes Badrutt offered to pay for their journey home if they didn't like what they found in winter. They did, and St Moritz has never looked back.

How long: 7 hours 30 minutes

SPIEZ–BRIG VIA KANDERSTEG (SWITZERLAND)

The opening of the 34.5-kilometre (21.5-mile) Lötschberg base tunnel in 2007 reduced the importance of this line, but because it serves the resorts of Adelboden (from Frutigen station) and Kandersteg and is such a scenic route, new trains with panoramic windows were built for the service between Bern, Spiez and Brig.

The 'old line' was never going to be easy to build, but there was a strong determination to create a railway between Bern and canton Valais through the immense mountain barrier at the south end of Kandertal. The railway from Spiez on Lake Thun reached Frutigen in 1901 and there it stopped while competing plans were assessed. In 1906 the Bern-Lötschberg-Simplon (BLS) company was formed and work began in the same year on the main challenge of tunnelling between Kandersteg and Goppenstein.

Picks and shovels were the tools at the beginning, but pneumatic drills were introduced in 1907. Disaster struck in July 1908 when water burst into the northern heading, bringing with it so much rock that within fifteen minutes the bore was filled for 1.5 kilometres (just under a mile) and 24 men lost their lives. The only course was to seal off the area with a wall 10 metres (33 feet) thick and divert the tunnel. Breakthrough on the new alignment came on 31 March 1911, and the railway was fully opened in 1913.

To allow the public to experience the railway at close quarters and enjoy the magnificent views at walking pace, BLS has created walks beside the north and south ramps to the Lötschberg Tunnel; the station at Kandersteg provides a free English translation of the information boards beside the Railway Adventure Trail.

Leaving Spiez, the line turns abruptly south east to enter Hondrich Tunnel, leading into the Kander Valley, with the characteristic pale green water of the glacial river on the right. Throughout the climb to Kandersteg, the railway offers progressively more impressive views of the peaks flanking

the valley, covered or fringed with snow for much of the year.

From Mülenen station a funicular ascends Niesen Kulm, beside which is the world's longest flight of steps – 11,674 of them, for maintenance workers. The views from the summit of Niesen are among the finest in the Bernese Oberland, and there is an attractive hotel at the summit that enables guests to see dawn over the Bernese Alps.

Construction of the base tunnel allowed water at 18°C to be fed from the rock to a newly built environmental attraction at Frutigen, providing an ideal habitat for Siberian sturgeon. So caviar is on the menu at Tropenhaus Frutigen (Tropical House), which demonstrates to visitors the potential of land-based aquaculture. Leaving Frutigen, the northern portal of the Lötschberg Base Tunnel can be seen and on the right are the ruins of Tellenburg Castle, which burned down in 1885.

The line then crosses an imposing viaduct before looping around the remains of Felsenburg Tower. The gradients steepen to 1 in 37 for much of the next 18 kilometres (11 miles) as the line describes two huge loops to gain the next step of the valley, using viaducts and tunnels to change direction.

On the platform at the delightful resort of Kandersteg is a small steam locomotive of 1911 used in the construction of the Lötschberg Tunnel. Car-carrying trains are operated through the tunnel to Goppenstein at the entrance to the beautiful Lötschental. The summit in the middle of the tunnel is the highest point reached by a standard-gauge adhesion (non-rack) railway in Switzerland, at 1,240 metres (4,068 feet).

The southern ramp descends at gradients as fierce as the northern counterpart along a ledge on the north flank of the Rhone Valley. Below is the main line from Geneva to Brig and beyond, a mass of mountain peaks stretching towards

Saas-Fee and the Matterhorn. It is difficult to appreciate the spectacular engineering of the railway from the train, but curves allow occasional glimpses of such structures as the great arc of steel forming the Bietschtal Bridge and the dramatic lattice girder Baltschieder Viaduct.

As the line drops down, the southern portal of the base tunnel and its junction with the railway from Geneva can be seen before arrival at the major interchange at Brig. Trains to Italy enter the Simplon Tunnel, and outside the main station are the metre-gauge trains of the Matterhorn Gotthard Bahn to take you to Zermatt or towards Chur and St Moritz.

How long: 1 hour

THE BERNINA EXPRESS (SWITZERLAND–ITALY)

It's a rather surreal experience watching the front of the train you are on heading in the opposite direction, as though you are in a toy train in Lilliput. But that is just one of the uncommon features of a journey in the far-from-Lilliputian Bernina Express, which runs from Chur and St Moritz to Tirano in Italy. Another feature is the chance to ride in open wagons between spring and autumn, which is ideal for photographers, and a noisy thrill clattering through the mostly unlined rock tunnels.

Like the Glacier Express, the Bernina Express relies purely on adhesion rather than a rack mechanism to scale the fearsome gradients – northbound trains have to overcome a vertical height of 1,827 metres (5,994 feet) in just 38 kilometres (23.6 miles) to reach the summit station of Ospizio Bernina, just below the pass, which is the highest rail crossing of the Alps at 2,257 metres (7,405 feet). It's just one of the reasons UNESCO made the railway a World Heritage Site. Though most people take the train to enjoy the dramatic changes in the mountain landscapes, there is reason to stop off at almost every station.

Bernina Express trains from Chur share the same route as the Glacier Express as far as Pontresina (see page 112). From St Moritz the train's panoramic coaches burrow through the Charnadüra II Tunnel as soon as the station in Switzerland's most ostentatious resort is left behind. Once through the tunnel, the train enters the curious area where two river valleys meet the dominant Inn Valley in the Upper Engadine. It is one of the few expanses of flattish ground and is overlooked by the tiny white-washed chapel of San Gion, picturesquely placed on a knoll with a solitary tree for company.

Turning abruptly south east, the line reaches the hillside resort of Pontresina, where Elizabeth Gaskell somehow managed to write *Wives and Daughters* while holidaying with her daughters in 1864. The walls of the Santa Maria parish church are entirely covered in frescoes, most notably eighteen almost completely preserved late 15th-century paintings of Mary Magdalene's life. From Pontresina, a horse-drawn carriage can take you through the larch and Arolla pine forest of Val Roseg.

When the railway opened as far as Morteratsch station in 1908, passengers could see the eponymous glacier; today it's a half-hour walk to reach it. Starting to climb, the train twists through the first of many hairpin bends and leaves the forest. For travellers with time to spare, a memorable diversion from Bernina Diavolezza station is the cablecar journey to the mountain hotel and restaurant at Diavolezza

(2,973 metres/9,754 feet) for a 'view of surpassing grandeur', as Baedecker quaintly put it. Even better, stay the night and rise before dawn to watch the sun break over the surrounding jumble of saw-toothed peaks and turn the snow a flamingo pink.

The train skirts the pale green waters of Lago Bianco and weaves its way along the shoreline, feet from the water's edge. Booted walkers are the only users of the summit station of Ospizio Bernina, where coarse grasses and stunted bushes grow among the rocks of the desolate plateau. The Italian builders of the railway had to be supplied by a twice-daily caravan of thirteen mules and three horses bringing up supplies from Poschiavo to their temporary huts.

The line descends through shelters protecting the sections most prone to avalanches or snow drifts and reaches the magnificently sited station at Alp Grüm. It's worth breaking the journey to have lunch or a hot chocolate on the station restaurant terrace overlooking the Palü Glacier in a great amphitheatre of rock.

Stand on the platform at Alp Grüm and the railway gives the illusion of falling off a cliff as the track drops away so steeply that ascending trains come over the brow like a bus over a humpback bridge. The views down Val Poschiavo are stupendous as the train describes a series of disorientating curlicues down the mountain through U-shaped curves. The train enters a tunnel and twists round inside the mountain to emerge in a different direction and glide over a chasm of fuming water.

Eventually the train emerges from the woods into upland meadows and arrives at the town of Poschiavo, the principal town of the small Italian-speaking enclave of Val Poschiavo. A maze of narrow streets surrounds the central piazza, water playing in its fountain and overlooked by several good

Photo: Hansueli Krapf

restaurants. Wander into the museum in Palazzo Mengotti and you may find ladies using historic looms to weave cloth for sale. To the south of the town is a row of handsome villas known as the Spanish quarter and built in about 1830 by returning hoteliers, brewers and pastrycooks, having made their money in Spain.

South of Poschiavo, passengers can feel rather superior as the train barges its way along the street, forcing puny cars to cower at the side of the road. At Le Prese the train passes the front door of an 1850s hotel beside a lake, a perfect setting for an Anita Brookner novel. Sheer walls of rock rise out of the water on the far side of the lake, and as the train passes Miralago station it takes another great dive for Italy, winding south over the final flourish – the spiral viaduct at Brusio, which allows the train to descend at such an incline that it loops under one of the arches. In the centre of the corkscrew, modern sculptures decorate the grass.

Orchards and market gardens flank the train as it clatters along the street, past front gardens and a tall campanile and across a square on the outskirts of Tirano, where Swiss trains terminate beside the Italian Railways' station. Among Tirano's historic streets are palm trees, making the Bernina Express one of the quickest transitions from glaciers to palm trees.

How long: 4 hours from Chur; 2 hours 20 minutes from St Moritz

CENTOVALLI (SWITZERLAND–ITALY)

International narrow-gauge lines are rare, and this 52-kilometre (32-mile) line is one of two between Switzerland

and Italy (see page 122 for the other). Linking Locarno in Switzerland with Domodossola in Italy, it takes its name from the hundred side valleys that the railway has to cross in its progress along the main valley of the River Melezza, entailing 83 bridges and viaducts. Its stations serve clustered villages of dark stone houses huddled round Italianate belfries, and the steep valley slopes are often covered in forests of larch or chestnut.

Construction started in 1913 on the Swiss side, but was interrupted by the First World War, and it was 25 November 1923 before the full line opened. The service is operated by the Ferrovie Autolinee Regionali Ticinesi, which uses its unfortunate acronym. The railway is a vital lifeline to many isolated communities as well as one of Switzerland's finest journeys for tourists. Nine of the twelve stations in Switzerland are request stops, often used by walkers on the numerous paths along the wooded slopes; intending passengers have to press a button in the shelter or, if there is none, to give a hand signal to the driver.

From either end, this glorious journey starts unpromisingly in a concrete bunker, the one in Locarno having a statue of the patron saint of miners, St Barbara. For the first few miles, the railway has the character of a modern tram, with two more underground stations before the train rushes up a steep gradient into the open. Soon after the first above-ground station at San Martino, the railway joins the River Maggia, which it follows to its confluence with the Melezza at Ponte Brolla. The gorge beneath the bridge contains a jumble of eroded rocks shaped like Henry Moore sculptures.

The line soon reaches Tegna, where the stuccoed villas have painted decoration that can be seen all along the valley. The tree-covered hills to the north rise higher and higher, bare patches of rock outcropping among the trees.

Photo: NAC

At Verscio, the church of San Fedele, topped by an octagonal tower, is clearly visible from the train just before the station. The 13th–14th-century building was rebuilt in 1743–8 into a lovely Baroque church with liberal use of marble.

The railway has climbed high above the river by Cavigliano, beyond which an immense bridge can be seen ahead; this steel structure, one of seventeen major bridges, leaps 91 metres (299 feet) across the River Isorno and is sufficiently high for bungee jumps. Intragna boasts the tallest bell-tower in Ticino, at 65 metres (213 feet), and near the station is the cablecar to Costa for a lovely walk through a walnut wood to Cremaso.

Beyond Intragna the valley becomes remoter and even more densely wooded, with an occasional farm in a clearing. The river can be glimpsed below, the banks periodically joined by stone arches with a shrine at the apex of their parapets. Waterfalls punctuate the great folds of hills that stretch into the distance, the intensity of their colour receding to a misty horizon. The trees are mostly deciduous, so the colours in autumn are spectacular.

Right by the station at the picturesque village of Verdasio is the cablecar up to the unspoilt hill village of Rasa, which is inaccessible to motor traffic. Leaving Verdasio, the views down to the river hundreds of feet below are breathtaking.

Some of the houses in the village of Palagnedra are decorated with paintings, and below the railway are the turquoise waters of an artificial lake that winds along the valley floor to Camedo, the last station in Switzerland and the site of another huge steel bridge on the eastern approach. At Camedo, the railway hires out bikes for a descent on two wheels to Ponte Brolla; since the road is at a much lower level than the railway, it gives a very different perspective.

Half a mile beyond Camedo, through a broader stretch of the valley, the railway comes to the border with the old road bridge on the right. Once in Italy, the line goes through a long stretch of shelters that interrupt views of the boulder-strewn river before the Vigezzo Valley opens out.

On a hillside above the large station at Re is the pilgrimage church and sanctuary of Madonna del Sangue, the destination of pilgrims for over 500 years since a fresco of the Madonna supposedly shed blood for 21 days after an enraged young man threw a stone at her forehead. The highest station on the line is reached at Santa Maria Maggiore, the largest community served by the railway. The village's popularity as a home for artists is evident from the number of galleries, and the square is bordered by some elegant palazzi. It has a tiny museum devoted to, of all things, chimney-sweeps. It was also the home of the inventor of Eau de Cologne, Giovanni Maria Farina (1685–1766).

Conifers replace deciduous trees and the hills diminish in height as the train presses west to the delightful village of Gagnone-Orcesco. The homogeneous character of the stone-walled buildings, usually roofed in stone too, is a feature of a succession of villages as the river threads through another gorge and the hillsides steepen. The natural beauty of this area is reflected in the name given to the valley, 'Valley of Painters'. After the pretty village of Marone, the line starts to descend, twisting down the contours to the first vines at Verigo.

Beyond Trontano the railway and the Val Vigezzo join the broad valley of the River Toce, Val Antigório, though the railway is still high above the valley floor, requiring a tortuous, flange-squealing descent through horseshoe curves to journey's end in the bunker at Domodossola, but with no St Barbara.

How long: 1 hour 45 minutes

BASTIA–AJACCIO (CORSICA)

Very little Corsican terrain lends itself to easy railway construction, so it is no surprise that all the railways of Corsica were built to metre gauge (3 feet 3 inches), though the traffic volumes were never likely to justify use of standard gauge. In common with many railway journeys, the principal line on Corsica offers views denied to all but intrepid mountain walkers.

After the greater part of the network was opened in 1888–94, it took until 1935 to complete a wonderfully scenic line along the east coast to Porto-Vecchio, which was so badly damaged during the Second World War that it was never rebuilt. This reduced the network from 360 to 231 kilometres (224 to 144 miles), but major investment in the 21st century has successfully revitalised services and produced impressive increases in passengers.

The line linking the two largest Corsican coastal towns cuts a diagonal swathe through the mountains of the centre, crossing one of Eiffel's lesser-known structures that spans the River Vecchio. The line used to be operated by articulated steam locomotives designed by Anatole Mallet, but today utilitarian, if much faster, railcars operate all services. Bastia station is only a few minutes' walk from the central Place St-Nicholas, the Genoese-built citadel and the old streets around the country's principal port.

It was from Bastia station that a locomotive was hijacked by a Russian vagabond in the 1930s; intent on getting to Ajaccio but lacking the fare, he commandeered an engine in steam and set off. Unfortunately, he was unaccustomed to the tight radius curves of Corsica, and the locomotive came off the rails at the first severe curve.

The journey's highlights begin with the steep-sided valley of the River Golo, with the first sightings of characteristically situated villages high up on the hillsides to escape the malarial mosquito, which was not eliminated until after the Second World War. At Corsica's only railway junction, Ponte Leccia, the line from the resort of Calvi trails in from the north.

The line starts to climb in earnest, and the first of many horseshoe loops comes after Francardo. Pale stone viaducts come thick and fast as the line constantly leaps across gullies and hurdles between hills.

Agriculture makes a brief appearance in the broader valleys leading to the old capital of Corte, as the train climbs through a series of horseshoe curves beneath slopes covered by the *maquis* for which the island is famous – a wonderfully aromatic mix of arbutus, juniper, laburnum, lavender, myrtle and rosemary, which gave its name to the resistance fighters during the Second World War.

Corte is a good place to break the journey to visit the imposing citadel and wander the labyrinth of cobbled alleys in search of lunch. The town was the Corsican capital during the 14-year Corsican Republic under the venerated Pasquale Paoli, who became a celebrated figure in Britain after his exile in 1795.

Continuing south west, the train clambers upward to give commanding views over unbroken forests. South of Venaco, flying buttresses brace the arched stone walls of a cutting before the engineering masterpiece of the line across the Vecchio. The bridge of three steel truss spans on stone piers was designed by Gustave Eiffel and built in 1890–4. Directly beneath it is a masonry arch of 1825–7, carrying the road. Though 80 metres high (262 feet), Eiffel's structure should ideally have been even higher, since trains have to dip down to it from both directions.

Photo: Michal Osmenda

Astonishing horseshoe curves help lift the line up the fierce gradients to Vivario station, where the water towers that replenished the tanks of steam locomotives can still be seen. Indicative of the climb and extent of the U-shaped curves, a straight line between kilometre posts 91 and 98 measures just 200 metres (656 feet).

The line runs high above the Vecchio Gorge, with vertiginous drops to the river. There is a glimpse of the hilltop ruins of Fort de Pasciolo, built by the French in 1770.

Laricio pine woods flank the 906-metre (2,972-foot) summit at Vizzavona station, where a restaurant and bar caters for the many walkers. From here the line descends continuously for 40 kilometres (25 miles) to Ajaccio, first through a dead-straight tunnel almost 4 kilometres (2.5 miles) long. The line twists and turns over more viaducts and through tunnels and chestnut forest to join the River Gravona, which the railway follows to the sea and the terminus in Corsica's largest town, where the house in which Napoleon was born in 1769 is the principal attraction.

How long: 3 hours 15 minutes

EL TRANSCANTABRICO (SPAIN)

The idea of using trains as mobile hotels to experience a country has proved extremely popular, and this historic narrow-gauge train provides a luxurious way to enjoy the landscapes and many of the most notable sights of northern Spain. The train of saloons and sleeping cars with en-suite shower-rooms operates eight-day excursions between

Santiago de Compostela, Bilbao and León (or vice versa) and four nights between Santiago de Compostela, Bilbao and San Sebastián. The train is stationary overnight and most meals other than breakfast are taken off the train; the price includes all meals and drinks with them.

Bilbao and its Guggenheim Museum apart, northern Spain is neglected in favour of the warmer and drier south – unless of course you are on pilgrimage. Santiago de Compostela has been the goal of pilgrims for over a millennium since the supposed discovery in 813 of the tomb of St James the Greater, a notion cleverly developed by the monks of Cluny. When Sir Francis Drake was marauding off the coast of Galicia and attacked La Coruna, Compostela's bishop was so afraid of losing the relics of St James that they were hidden – all too well, since their whereabouts were forgotten and only rediscovered in 1879.

So the city's Parador Reyes Católicos is an appropriately historic place for the train's passengers to rendezvous, since the huge building was created around four courtyards in the late 15th century for poor pilgrims to stay. It overlooks the vast Praza do Obradoiro and the famous granite cathedral, whose Romanesque core acts as an improbably good foil for the later baroque embellishments.

After a sumptuous four-course lunch in the Parador's great dining-room, guests are taken to the start of the train journey at El Ferrol by the coach that shadows the train for sightseeing excursions. Covering about 1,000 kilometres (621 miles) in eight days, the pace is leisurely with seldom more than three hours' train travel a day, leaving plenty of time for sightseeing, long lunches and Spain's customarily late dinners.

Eucalyptus forests dominate the early part of the journey when the train periodically turns inland to avoid bridging

Photo: DavidfGB

one of the many *rías* (estuaries) that punctuate the Bay of Biscay. For long stretches the train is close to the rollers crashing on to the rocky coastline, the gorse covering the foreshore bright with yellow flowers. Among the farms are the elevated racks for drying corn known as *hórreos*, whose roofs are sometimes decorated with tiny pyramids at the corners and ridge ends.

The first evening visit is to the walled town of Viveiro, overlooking its harbour. It is the first of many northern Spanish towns to share with Malta a love of two- or even three-storeyed balconied windows from first-floor level upwards, though in Viveiro the *solanas* often cover the whole façade of the house to suck in as much light as possible. Alan Jay Lerner was clearly unfamiliar with Galicia when he wrote the lyrics of *My Fair Lady* about the rain in Spain staying mainly on the plain; the region endures heavy rainfall and many days when light is at a premium.

Passengers take to the water at Viveiro for a boat trip along the Mariña Lucense estuary, passing fishing boats specialising in line-caught hake, before pressing eastwards to Ribadeo. Shale pillars of rock rearing out of the sea form the nearby Praia das Catedrais Natural Monument, its clifftop heather spanned by raised boardwalks. From Ribadeo the train heads inland along a particularly lovely stretch following the saltmarshes of the Eo estuary, flanked by gently rising slopes of pasture and woods, until the water narrows into a ribbon that the railway can cross with ease and return along the opposite bank towards the sea.

The Chapel of the White Virgin and cemetery adjacent to the lighthouse above Luarca must be one of Spain's most spectacularly sited churches and burial grounds, perched on a high peninsula with long views along the cliffs in each direction. Below, the white houses of the tuna-fishing port huddle round the cove. Continuing through Asturias, the apple blossom is a harbinger of the rough cider guests are invited to sample in Oviedo after a visit to the exceptional early 9th-century pre-Romanesque church of San Julián de los Prados. The basilican-plan church was used in the filming of *Vicky Cristina Barcelona* by Woody Allen and starring Penélope Cruz, Javier Bardem and Scarlett Johansson.

In the Picos de Europa, passengers are taken to the symbolic birthplace of the *reconquista* at Covadonga, where the site of the first Christian victory over the Moors, probably in 722, is marked by a basilica housing a statue of Our Lady of Covadonga (the Virgin Mary), patron of Asturias. Another pilgrimage chapel is visited on a hill above the harbour town of Llanes, sitting in a small cove against the dramatic backdrop of the Cantabrian Mountains; the chapel and an elaborate annual ceremony and dance venerate San Roque and his dog.

For many the highlight is the brilliantly re-created caves and paintings of Altamira near the medieval village of Santillana del Mar. They were the first prehistoric cave paintings to be discovered, in 1879. Because of the damage done by carbon dioxide in the breath of visitors, the original caves were closed in 2002 to save the 14,500-year-old originals depicting bison, horses and deer from further deterioration. Despite creating an exact replica, the government reopened the original in 2010, against all scientific and conservation advice.

At the other extreme, Frank Gehry's Guggenheim Museum in Bilbao showed what an exciting modern building can do to transform the reputation and fortunes of a city. The supporting cast of other structures includes underground stations by Norman Foster, a bridge by Santiago Calatrava and Europe's largest indoor market, of 1929, where the El

Transcantabrico's guests are taken to admire the magnificent cornucopia from the sea. León Cathedral, regarded as the finest example of the French Gothic style in Spain, is a worthy conclusion to the tour.

How long: 8 days

AL ANDALUS (SPAIN)

The clink of champagne glasses is always a good way to start a social occasion, and the reception in the lounge car of the Al Andalus before departure from Seville's Santa Justa station is no exception. Guests from half a dozen countries soon find their linguistic groups and after half an hour of chat head for the dining car and an introduction to Andalusian cuisine.

This slow way to see some of the architectural and natural highlights of Andalusia, and other parts of western Spain began operation in 1985, using 1929–30 carriages rebuilt to provide the amenities and sense of period opulence that would attract an international clientele. The train takes its name from the caliphate that at its peak in 1085 encompassed most of what is now Spain and Portugal. The train's brown and cream lounge, dining and sleeping cars can accommodate up to 64 people, all enjoying en-suite facilities within the generous coach dimensions allowed by the wider Iberian track gauge of 5 feet 6 inches (1,676 mm).

Lunch on the first day gives an idea of the gastronomic delights to come: a cream soup of porcini with dessert sherry followed by cod in puff pastry stuffed with ratatouille and ginger, local sirloin marinated in raspberries, and chocolate cake with cream-cheese ice-cream. A journey on the Al Andalus is no time for weight watching.

A shadowing road coach meets the train at Córdoba station for the first of many excursions with local expert guides. The old city, and especially what was the Jewish quarter, is made up of a labyrinth of alleyways and passages. Tens of thousands of Jews as well as Christians once lived here in harmony with the Muslim rulers. The narrow lanes were designed to provide shade from the sun, and even the patterned pebble floors of courtyards were made impermeable so that water splashing from a fountain would evaporate and cool the air.

The alleys are an incongruous way to approach one of the world's most astounding buildings, the Great Mosque begun in 785 into which a cathedral has been inserted. The forest of 856 columns and double arches is so confusing and dense that it seems infinite, and the sense of a palm-tree forest must have soothed those homesick for Damascus from where the Caliphate came.

The Al Andalus's clockwise tour takes in a few small towns, such as Baeza and its olive oil museum and Úbeda with its remarkable underground 14th-century synagogue, as well as the autonomous community's principal cities of Grenada, Cadiz, Ronda and Jerez de la Frontera. During the week guests enjoy flamenco dancing and song, equestrian arts, a boat ride along the Guadalquivir River for a walk among the sand dunes, juniper and stone pines of Doñana National Park, a visit to Spain's oldest bullring in Ronda, and a final tour of Seville.

Though urban Spain is the focus of the visits, the journeys between them give plenty of opportunity to appreciate the landscape, often dominated by undulating hills of olive

Photo: André Marques

trees stretching to the horizon, interrupted by white-walled villages flecked with oleander and bougainvillea. Vines and sunflowers also thrive in the khaki-coloured soil, and the dark rocks of the Sierra Morena ridges provide a striking backdrop.

The tour makes it easy to see how the American writer Washington Irving became so captivated with Andalusia and Grenada in particular that he spent three months in 1829 living in the Alhambra, and wrote *Tales of the Alhambra* while living in London.

How long: 6 days

GOLDEN EAGLE DANUBE EXPRESS (BALKANS AND EASTERN EUROPE)

In 2014 Golden Eagle Luxury Trains took over the Danube Express, which had begun operation with a train of rebuilt Hungarian carriages in 2011. The deluxe accommodation is generously sized, with five en-suite cabins per carriage, while the Heritage sleeper is a cut above the style of sleeping cars that were once such a familiar part of the European continent. Though operating a varied programme of tours through the Balkans and Eastern Europe, with off-train visits on foot and by coach, the train deserves inclusion in a pantheon of great journeys for the quality of the experiences it offers.

How long: 3–8 days

AFRICA

ROVOS RAIL (PRETORIA–CAPE TOWN)

In an age when bland corporate giants homogenise our globalised planet, there is something reassuring in finding that individual passion and determination can still create something as fine as Rovos Rail's luxury train. The brainchild of Rohan Voss, it began operation in 1989 and has remained very much a family business. Attention to detail has been the abiding hallmark of the train, providing the smallest tweak to the service that would improve the passenger's experience.

The train of period dining-cars, lounge cars, observation cars and all en-suite sleeping cars operates a variety of tours through southern Africa with all meals, beverages and off-train excursions included. Itineraries venture as far as Dar es Salaam in Tanzania and Swakopmund in Namibia, but the most frequent route is between Cape Town and Pretoria. Most trains begin or end at Rovos Rail's own Capital Park station near Pretoria.

A sense of occasion is created by a champagne reception held before departure in the elegant lounge of the large colonial-style station at Capital Park, which resembles a five-star hotel lounge rather than a station waiting room. The site covers 24 hectares (59 acres) and includes the workshops where the carriages and semi-retired steam locomotives are maintained. For railway buffs there is a small railway museum and semaphore signals to recall the heyday of South African Railways.

A mid-afternoon departure gives everyone time to get to

know one another over high tea, served in the lounge and observation cars as the train rolls through the goldfields of the Witwatersrand. High tea implies a waiving of dinner, but a gong summons guests for a 7.30pm five-course dinner with a different South African wine for each course – this is another journey to suspend weight-watching. The menu favours traditional dishes such as game, and fresh local ingredients are used wherever possible.

The border between the maize lands of western Transvaal and the Orange Free State is crossed during the night, the train paralleling the course of the Orange River as it heads for the diamond fields of Kimberley and an arrival after breakfast. The train pauses for guests to visit the Big Hole and its diamond mine museum, which leave an indelible impression. The viewing platform jutting out over the world's biggest excavation can induce vertigo, as you gaze down 175 metres (574 feet) to the turquoise water filling the hole, which has a circumference of 1.6 kilometres (1 mile). De Beers gave a huge sum to turn the Big Hole into a world-class tourist destination, and a film gives a factual account of the development of the mine from 1871 and conditions for those who worked it. The mine is also the theme of Wilbur Smith's novel *Men of Men*.

High tea is on the table by arrival at the important railway junction and livestock town of De Aar, which was one of the last great centres of steam power in South Africa, providing the huge Class 25NC 4-8-4 locomotives that operated freights over the line to Kimberley. Photographers from all over the world were attracted to the line to record trains over the country's busiest steam line, which was nicknamed the 'Steel Kyalami' after the country's motor-racing circuit near Johannesburg – the line's relatively straight alignment allowed speeds over 112 km/h (70 mph) until a clampdown

Photo: David Brossard

in 1973. The fastest time recorded was in 1961, when a locomotive and single coach covered the 235 kilometres (146 miles) at an average speed of 96 km/h (60 mph) to take a severely injured shunter to hospital in Kimberley.

Dinner is likely to distract attention from the village of Merriman, named after a son of Street in Somerset who became the last Prime Minister of Cape Colony before the formation of the Union of South Africa in 1910. During the night the train bowls through Beaufort West, the 'Capital of the Karoo' and famous as the home of the young Christian Barnard, who performed the world's first successful heart transplant in 1967. Also passed in the dark are abandoned blockhouses from the Second Boer War, one of the best-preserved being that guarding the Geelbeks River bridge between Beaufort West and Matjiesfontein. Rudyard Kipling wrote a poem about the loneliness and tedium of defending one, in 'Bridge-Guard in the Karroo'.

The stop next morning at Matjiesfontein is an extraordinary experience. The isolated settlement was founded by a Scottish railwayman, James Douglas Logan, who began his South African career carrying bags at Cape Town station before creating this oasis in the Karoo. He planted trees and built the Lord Milner Hotel, today superbly preserved as a comfortable time warp with original and antique furniture. As Olive Schreiner, author of *The Story of an African Farm*, wrote in 1890, 'It is curious and to me very attractive, this mixture of civilization and the most wild untamed freedom; the barren mountains and the wild Karoo and the railway train…'.

A London double-decker bus ferries visitors from the 1890 station around the tidy streets and the attractions, which include a collection of well-restored railway carriages, an 1893 Glasgow-built steam locomotive and a railway museum with signalling lever frame. The collection includes two Royal Daimlers from George VI's tour of South Africa in 1947, when he was accompanied by Princesses Elizabeth (now Queen Elizabeth II) and Margaret. Another museum contains all manner of bygones that Olive Schreiner might have known when she was living in Matjiesfontein in 1890–92. The town's quiet atmosphere makes it hard to imagine that during the Boer War 10,000 soldiers were based here with 20,000 horses on the surrounding land.

As the train heads south west, the peculiarity of Matjiesfontein becomes all the more evident as the desolation and size of the Karoo continues to unfold. Among the sage bushes and eucalyptus trees, any evidence of human habitation – rusting agricultural implements or a wind-vaned pump – is without a sign of life. The barren Great Karoo morphs into the Little Karoo, and the serrated grey mountains that divide it from the vineyards and orange groves of the coastal plain come into view. The Karoo finally comes to an end as the train weaves through the Hex River tunnels, from which the train emerges into the fertile Hex River Valley.

This lush country grows most of the table grapes, as well as the varieties for South Africa's wines. White Dutch-gabled houses stand among the vines at the end of long avenues in the country around Paarl, the largest town of the wine region where Huguenot settlers established the first vineyards in the late 17th century. The Cape Flat dunes contoured by Atlantic winds give way to the green suburbs of Cape Town and the immensity of Table Mountain and its neighbouring peaks, sometimes skimmed by a thin layer of cloud known as the 'tablecloth'.

The journey ends in the unremarkable modern terminus, slightly redeemed by a plinth in the concourse with South

Africa's first steam locomotive, a diminutive tank locomotive built by Hawthorns & Company of Leith in Scotland in 1859. It arrived with William Dabbs, who put it into operation and drove the locomotive for as long as it was in use with the Cape Town Railway & Dock Company. His contribution to the town was commemorated in a street named after him.

How long: 2–14 days

ASIA

GOLDEN EAGLE TRANS-SIBERIAN EXPRESS (RUSSIA)

The idea of the world's longest train journey captures the imagination like no other: crossing seven time zones and almost a hundred degrees of latitude, seeing for oneself the vastness of the Russian forests and the railway that has played such a powerful role in the country's history, has attracted generations of travellers. As Eric Newby wrote, all other journeys, even the longer ones in North America, are 'peanuts'.

But there is no getting away from the unsurprising fact that hours of birch and conifers pall, that parts of the journey are boring and a good opportunity to read some of those weighty Russian novels. Even one of the supposed highlights, the Ural Mountains, are an anticlimax. Those remembering the moment in the film of Pasternak's *Doctor Zhivago* when, travelling in goods wagons to Yuriatin, Zhivago and his son

Sasha first glimpse the Urals, will be disappointed by the reality – they were described by Colin Thubron as 'a faint upheaval of pine-darkened slopes'. Though most of the film's railway sequences were made in Spain, the 'Urals' were shot in Canada.

So taking a service train without breaks at cities along the way may appeal to those wanting an 'authentic' experience, entailing much fraternisation with fellow passengers, some of whom will view varying degrees of alcohol consumption as the only antidote to the journey's longueurs. Most will favour interrupting the journey or taking one of the tourist trains over the route, the Tsars Gold or the more luxurious Golden Eagle Trans-Siberian Express. This 21-car train was launched in April 2007 by Prince Michael of Kent and provides comfort unknown since Tsarist times – with the benefit of modern plumbing in the form of en-suite power showers, DVD players and individually controlled air conditioning in the Gold and Silver class cabins, as well as lounge and dining cars.

Cost aside, one's choice may be determined by route: for example, both tourist trains run via Kazan, allowing passengers to visit the magnificent Kremlin, ringed by 2 kilometres (1.24 miles) of white walls punctuated by conical-roofed towers; service trains do not. Then there is the option of destination: Vladivostok, the longest journey at 9,289 kilometres (5,772 miles), or Beijing via either Manchuria or Mongolia.

The Golden Eagle departs from Kazansky station, whose entrance-hall ceiling is a sky of cavorting fighter planes and airships – though begun in 1913, the station was not finished until 1940. Service trains for the Far East leave from Yaroslavsky terminus, Moscow's busiest station with a quirky façade of 1902–4 in a neo-Russian Revival style designed by

Fyodor Schechtel, who was Russia's pre-eminent master of art nouveau.

From either station, Moscow's suburbs seem interminable, but eventually dreary apartment blocks are exchanged for the first forests and glimpses of wooden dachas among the trees. The train carves through the seemingly limitless forests of Russia, a rolling panorama of silver birch and pine broken by the occasional village or town. Inured to ostentatious displays of wealth by Russian oligarchs in western Europe, it comes as a shock to realise that an early traveller over the Trans-Siberian would see little difference in the remoter places; corrugated iron may have replaced thatch on roofs, but the small single-storey dwellings of bare wood weathered grey are still surrounded by ramshackle wood fences and roads of mud. The best-kept places are the cemeteries, gaudy with plastic flowers, among the silver birch woods.

The domes above Vladimir's roofline belong to the city's Assumption Cathedral. Vladimir was politically the most important city in Russia in the 12th century and is one of the Golden Ring cities containing outstanding architecture from the 12th–18th centuries.

The city that briefly took the surname of the playwright Maxim Gorky has reverted to Nizhny Novgorod; founded in 1221, it is worth a break to see the wooden buildings of the old city, centred on two pedestrianised streets.

Forest gives way to fields before the major junction of Kotelnich, and the first cuttings of the journey denote the beginnings of the Urals. A copper-smelting works set up in the 1720s was behind the foundation of Perm, which is referred to as Yuriatin in *Doctor Zhivago*. Regarded as the gateway to the Urals, it is also an old centre of intellectual life (it's twinned with Oxford) and has fine galleries and museums. The old town has some attractive secular and ecclesiastical buildings in styles from the baroque to art nouveau.

East of Perm is the railway's highest point in the Urals, which barely reaches 500 metres (1,640 feet) but offers much broader views across the tree tops. At kilometre post 1,777, an obelisk flashes past the window, marking the transition from Europe to Asia at the continental division.

Russia's fourth largest city, Ekaterinburg, will be forever associated with the murder of the former Tsar Nicholas II and his family during the night of 16–17 July 1918 in the mansion of an engineer named Ipatiev, where they had been imprisoned since the end of April, over a year after Nicholas's forced abdication. A new church has been built on the site of the Ipatiev House, which the local party boss Boris Yeltsin demolished in 1977 on Brezhnev's orders for fear of it becoming a place of pilgrimage, which it now has. The site has been built over by the wonderfully named Church on the Blood in the Name of All Saints of the Russian Land, which was consecrated in 2003. It is a traditional Russian Orthodox church building, and incorporates the site of the basement room, where bullets ricocheted off the many diamonds that had been sewn into the undergarments of the female Romanovs, into a soulless cream-coloured space with an immensely tall ceiling. Nearby is an iconostasis of white porcelain framing the paintings of saints.

Siberia officially begins at kilometre post 2,102, and the region is unlikely to shed its association with exile by road or rail and the Gulag forced-labour camps, searingly portrayed by Solzhenitsyn's *One Day in the Life of Ivan Denisovich* and *The Gulag Archipelago*. Founded in 1586, the Trans-Siberian town of Tyumen is the oldest Russian settlement in Siberia and was notorious as the site of one of the forwarding prisons for convicts on their way into exile further east.

Photo: Sergey Prokudin-Gorsky

A 650-metre (2,133-foot) bridge on pillars of Ural Mountain granite carries the railway over the River Irtysh and into Omsk. This was the White Army headquarters during the Civil War; the former headquarters of Admiral Kolchak, the White Russian leader, is now a fine arts museum. It was east along the Trans-Siberian that he fled in a series of special trains in November 1919, carrying 9,072 kilograms (20,000 pounds) of the Imperial Gold Reserve. Soon after, the railway became so choked with trains that their freezing occupants burnt them to keep warm while waiting for help that never came.

East of Omsk the railway crosses the Baraba Steppe, a green plain broken up by shallow lakes. Shortly before Novosibirsk the line crosses the 870-metre (2,854-foot) Great Ob River Bridge, its piers designed to deflect ice. Founded in 1893, Siberia's largest city is built with a rare sense of space and boasts the world's largest opera house and a red-brick cathedral completed in 1898. Its peppermint-coloured station of 1929–41 is the starting point for excursions into the celebrated beauty of the Altai Mountains, and the city has many museums, including the History Museum of the Western Siberian Railway.

After a stretch in the taiga, twisting around hills with clusters of log cabins, the train reaches Krasnoyarsk, which Chekhov thought the most beautiful city in Siberia, dating from 1628. He would not recognise much of it, apart from the old town on a hill and its restored Annunciation Cathedral of 1802–12. Soon after leaving Krasnoyarsk the line crosses the Yenisey River on a 1-kilometre (1,094-yard) viaduct that opened in 1999.

Timber mills and open-cast mining disfigure the hills before Tayshet, junction for the Baikal–Amur Mainline (BAM), which was built as a strategic alternative to the

Trans-Siberian Railway and runs 600–1,000 kilometres (373–621 miles) north of the Trans-Siberian through taiga, mountain tundra and wide valleys. Construction of the BAM was begun in the 1930s with forced labour and finally completed in 1991, with full opening through to Sovetskaya Galan on the Pacific Ocean. Intrepid travellers sometimes choose this more northerly route.

The Trans-Siberian winds through the foothills of the Sayan Mountains. Before Irkutsk, the taiga thins and the country flattens out. The city's grand station of 1898 is an appropriate introduction to a place once known as the 'Paris of Siberia', which still has some fine Neo-classical buildings and characteristic wooden buildings with frilly fretwork decoration.

Irkutsk is the gateway for excursions to Lake Baikal, where winter ice is so thick that before the railway was built through the difficult hilly countryside along the edge, tracks were laid on it in winter for the trains heading further east. Unfortunately, a spot warmed slightly by a hot spring caused a locomotive to break through the ice and plunge into the depths below, where it remains.

Before the railway around Lake Baikal was completed, trains were carried for 640 kilometres on the ice-breaking train ferry SS *Baikal*, built in 1897 in Newcastle-upon-Tyne by Armstrong, Whitworth. Manufactured in just six months, the components of the 4,250-ton vessel formed over 7,000 crates and were shipped to St Petersburg, loaded on to railway wagons and delivered to the then eastern railhead at Krasnoyarsk for the final part of the journey – over 1,280 kilometres (795 miles) by horse-drawn sledges and carts and by river to the lake. Some parts took two years to arrive, and it was alleged that many were stolen en route. The boilers weighing in at 20 tons were a particular challenge. The vessel was assembled on the lake shore by workers sent out from Newcastle. When the Circum-Baikal Railway was completed in 1904, the *Baikal* was kept in reserve until destroyed during the Russian Civil War. A smaller sister ship, the *Angara*, survives as a museum piece in Irkutsk.

The section after Irkutsk is one of the most scenic parts of the whole route, traversing the Primorsky Mountains with glimpses of the lake before descending to run beside the water for nearly 200 kilometres (124 miles). Despite worsening pollution, the world's largest freshwater lake remains a natural wonder with two-thirds of its 1,700 species of flora and fauna unique to the 25 million-year-old lake.

The great ballet dancer Rudolf Nureyev was born on a train in 1938 as it skirted Lake Baikal while his mother made the six-day trip from her Urals village to join her husband, a soldier and dedicated communist, in Russia's Far East.

Mysovaya is the port on the eastern shore once served by the *Baikal* and *Angara*. Skirting a mountain range with views of extinct volcanoes, the line leaves the lake to follow the Selenga River valley all the way to Ulan-Ude, renowned for its vast bronze head of Lenin. Besides having an impressive open-air museum of reconstructed Buryat buildings, the town is the junction for the Mongolian route to Beijing.

Passing conifer-covered mountains and crossing cattle-grazed plains, the train arrives at the railway settlement of Mogocha and its notoriously brutal climate with extremes of −60°C in winter and intense summer sun. After the end of the taiga, the railway reaches an area that serves as the granary for eastern Russia. Shortly before Khabarovsk, the last major town before Vladivostok, the line crosses the longest bridge on the entire Trans-Siberian. The 3,890-metre (4,254-yard) bridge carries railway and road over the Amur River.

Firs and pines are replaced by deciduous trees as the train turns south through hilly country, wide valleys, alpine scenery and finally pastoral hills before the Pacific comes into view and arrival in Vladivostok, strikingly located on coastal hills. Vladivostok station is based on Moscow's Yaroslavsky station, with wall mosaics of horsemen, birds, berries and fruits, an ornate ceiling mural and tiled floor. Off-limits for decades, the reason can be found in the military and naval subjects of many of the city's museums.

How long: 11–22 days

THE WORLD'S HIGHEST PASSENGER SERVICE (CHINA)

The railway into Tibet was one of the most controversial railways of recent years, for environmental as well as political reasons, though no amount of opposition would have prevented China building the railway to Lhasa. A railway to Tibet was included in Dr Sun Yat-sen's 1917–20 railway plan for 100,000 kilometres (62,137 miles) of new railway. The 1,142-kilometre (710-mile) railway from Golmud to Lhasa opened in 2006 and includes the highest section of railway in the world, reaching 5,072 metres (16,640 feet) at the Tangula Pass.

After leaving the previous terminus at Golmud, reached in 1984, the views across broad empty grassland of the Kunlan Mountains and snow-covered peaks grow steadily more impressive as the powerful diesel locomotives growl their way into the rarefied air that requires emergency oxygen supplies

Photo © Michel Royon

to be carried in the train. You know it's a serious concern because this country of endemic smoking has banned it beyond Golmud, and there's no rice for lunch because the altitude makes it impossible to boil water. Climbing through horseshoe curves and some of the country's longest tunnels, the railway crosses 675 bridges, straddling wide valleys of ochre-coloured sandstone on impressive concrete structures still unweathered by freezing temperatures.

Herds of black-coated horned yaks and wild asses are a common feature of the vast, wide landscape, though a glimpse of the increasingly endangered Tibetan antelope is rare. A scenic highlight of the journey is Cuona Lake, which is generally frozen and glints in sunshine. But perhaps the most extraordinary and humbling sight can be pilgrims on their way to Lhasa, progressing on foot and performing repeated prostrations, with pads to protect their hands and knees. Barren hillsides are occasionally punctuated by farmhouses with projecting wooden verandas or four-corner pinnacles.

Although there is a descent into Lhasa, four-fifths of the railway from Golmud is over 4,000 metres (13,123 feet) and half its length is laid on permafrost. The last section is across grassland with progressively more activity in the fields and on the roads. Lhasa station's architecture has echoes of the White Palace part of the Potala Palace; this majestic structure begun in 1645 remains the city's main attraction, despite its obsolete role as the home of the Dalai Lama.

How long: 13 hours 30 minutes

NEW JALPAIGURI–DARJEELING (INDIA)

The Darjeeling Himalayan Railway (DHR) has been described as the most famous narrow-gauge railway in the world and has achieved a fame out of all proportion to its size and economic value. Its magnificent location and 'toy trains', as they are constantly described, have captured the imagination of people across the world and encouraged them to visit this relatively remote part of India.

Climate is central to Darjeeling's story. Were it not for the contrast it afforded with the heat of the plains and Calcutta in particular, it would never have been developed in the way it has. As the provincial governor Sir Olaf Caroe put it: 'I don't think there is anything in life which is such a relief and such a physical delight as going from the heat of the plains in the hot weather up into the mountains, gradually feeling it getting cooler.'

But for today's visitor, it is the combination of spectacular scenery, venerable steam locomotives and inventive civil engineering that makes the railway so appealing. The DHR was the first major narrow-gauge railway in India and the very first to be built using capital raised within the country. For these and other reasons, UNESCO considered it and other hill station railways in India to be worthy of World Heritage Site status.

Construction of the 82-kilometre (51-mile) line began in 1879, opening in stages with a formal opening of the full line by the Lieutenant-Governor of Bengal, Sir Ashley Eden, in July 1881. It played a crucial role in allowing civil servants to spend the summer in the hill station, as well as in providing transport for the schools, sanatoria, tea plantations and military establishments along the route.

The journey begins at New Jalpaiguri, where broad-gauge trains from Kolkata (Calcutta) terminate. After Siliguri, the railway enters the region known as the terai, once forest infested with mosquitoes and more agreeable wildlife such as elephants and tigers, but now replaced in many parts with tea plantations.

At Sukna station, where an upstairs room has a display of historic photographs, trains used to be divided into several portions for the steeper climbs ahead, following one another up the hill. Mark Twain, who found the journey 'so wild and interesting and exciting and enchanting that it ought to take a week', wrote that a message was once sent from Sukna station: 'Tiger eating stationmaster on front porch; telegraph instructions.' Whether apocryphal or not, a tiger was certainly found lounging in the shade at Sukna in 1900, and 15 years later a tiger sleeping in a culvert was startled by a train and, in its hurry to flee from the shrieking monster, knocked over a farmer.

As the bark from the locomotive testifies, the climb begins straightaway as the line starts its sinuous course into the hills, flanked by forest of bamboo, the hardwood sal, toona and screw-pines. Sightings from the train often included leopards, wild buffalo, deer, hogs, elephants, cheetah and panthers, and on occasions cylinder drain cocks have been used to emit a conical cloud of steam to try to dislodge or scare an obdurate elephant. Elephants can still be seen, and wires are strung between trees at vulnerable points to keep them away from the line.

The railway climbs the hill with the help of six reverses and three spiral loops. Frequent stops for water allow passengers to descend to acquaint themselves with the sounds and smell of the forest or to admire the views. After the idyllically sited station at Rangtong, the vegetation becomes denser, with creepers hanging between trees.

As the train leaves the first loop at Chunbatti, spectacular views open up over the plains below. The railway's workshops at Tindharia can be seen on a promontory high above the line long before the train reaches the place, and similarly an ascending train could be heard for at least half an hour before it arrived. Before Tindharia, the railway scores five levels of track into the slopes of Selim Hill and negotiates two zig-zags in quick succession.

At a point where the line curves round the hillside on which Tindharia stands, higher up, local boys used to jump off and race up the hill with orders for refreshments, knowing the train would take another half hour to reach the station, so long is the climb by an elongated U.

Road and railway describe a horseshoe as they cling to the hillside, the railway climbing to another reverse, its upper level close to the children's home of Santa Shawan, founded by Mother Teresa. It was on the train to Darjeeling on 10 September 1946, while returning for her annual retreat from the Loreto Convent in Calcutta, that Mother Teresa had the 'call within a call' to start the Missionaries of Charity in Calcutta.

The train passes close to an enchanting group of Buddhist stupas before the second loop, which became known as 'Agony Point' and required a huge amount of earthmoving to create the formation. There are magnificent distant views for much of the way to Kurseong, looking back over the route of the railway. The passage of a curved cutting through the rocks of Giddapahar (the Jackal's Hill) marks a dramatic change of landscape with more mountain ranges coming into view and tea estates covering many of the slopes. Furious whistling to encourage the removal of pop-up stalls on the track precedes arrival at the largest and

Photo: Mjanich

most important intermediate station, Kurseong, which is arranged as a terminus.

So after the fire is raked and water taken, the train leaves Kurseong by backing out of the terminus and resuming its course, passing through the bazaar so close to stalls that one can smell the aromas of spices. The novel sights of Buddhist monasteries and prayer poles are matched by changes in vegetation as the hillsides are clothed in rhododendron and mountain dahlias, and firs introduced from Japan tower over chestnut, cherry, willow and pear trees.

The forests that once covered the slopes have been heavily thinned, though walnuts, laurels, magnolias, rhododendrons, oak and chestnut still grow on them. As the train curls round a Tibetan gompa with golden stupas, Kanchenjunga comes into view for the first time. The mountain was first climbed in 1955, by two British climbers who adhered to a promise followed by all subsequent climbs that they would respect the veneration of the mountain by local people and stop just short of the summit.

The railway's summit and the highest railway station in India is reached at Ghum, at 2,258 metres (7,408 feet), where the train charges straight through the bazaar. Above Ghum is Tiger Hill, which offers the district's best view of Everest, the world's highest mountain. Named after the Welshman Col. Sir George Everest (1790–1866), the Surveyor General of India, the mountain will forever be associated with the fatal attempted ascent in 1924 by George Mallory and Andrew Irvine.

The railway descends towards Darjeeling along the Little Rungeet river valley, threading a cutting that called for the first use of a snowplough in India, in 1882–3, when snow drifted into it. The railway passes underneath the sole surviving aerial ropeway bringing tea up from the valley for transport to the plains.

The journey ends at the Art Deco station built in 1944, close to the bazaar that Mark Twain found 'worth coming from Calcutta to see, even if there were no Kinchinjunga and Everest'. The station's two-storey structure is enveloped by a concrete roof, which Twain thought more suited to being 'the restaurant of a holiday camp in Bognor Regis' than a station in the Himalayas, though even this questionable period piece has been disfigured by an ugly office block dumped across the station in 1980.

Unfortunately a sentence of Sir Ashley Eden's speech at the opening of the DHR has proved prophetic: 'It is not expected that we shall never hear of any more landslips or temporary obstructions or other mishaps unavoidable on a hill road.' He was unduly sanguine when he expressed the view that 'with the large train establishment of the Company and its appliances, these obstructions will be affairs of hours instead of days'. Landslips have been an almost annual occurrence, some so severe that new alignments have had to be built and services suspended for months, so it is wise to check the current position before planning a visit.

How long: 6 hours 15 minutes

THE MAHARAJAS' EXPRESS (INDIA)

India has embraced the hotel-train concept more enthusiastically than any other country. Five ribbons of pampered luxury with sleeping, dining, lounge and bar cars weave varying itineraries, with off-train excursions by coach to places of historic, architectural and natural interest. All

Photo: Simon Pielow

offer generous-sized bedrooms with full en-suite shower-rooms, thanks to the wide coach dimensions permitted by the 5-foot 6-inch (1,676-mm) track gauge. Many choose trains for safety (141,000 people died in crashes on Indian roads in 2014) as well as the convivial pleasures of cosmopolitan company – there are usually at least half a dozen nationalities on board.

The Indian Panorama itinerary of the Maharajas' Express begins as many tours do in Delhi, with dinner served on the way to Jaipur. Asia's first planned city was founded by the astrologer, mathematician and warrior Sawai Jai Singh, and the first day is spent visiting his extraordinary observatory of 1728, the only one of the five he built which is still operational, as well as his old capital palace at Amber. Almost every surface in this fusion of Mughal and Rajput architecture is adorned by carving, mirrors, precious stones or painted decoration. Guests take turns in playing a chukka from the top of a mahout-guided elephant on the Maharaja of Jaipur's polo field, each goal being celebrated by a noisy fanfare from a colourful troupe of uniformed brass and percussion musicians.

Each of the eight day-tours has a couple of visits: to the famous tiger reserve at Ranthanbore; the fabulous abandoned city of Fatehpur Sikri, which had to be given up when the water supply failed just fifteen years after completion; the Taj Mahal; the medieval fort palace of Orchha; the temples at Khajuraho, famed for their erotic couplings, though they cover only a small part of the stones; the ghats at Varanasi; the residency at Lucknow and the city's monumental 18th-century Great Imambara, built as a famine-relief project.

Between the visits there is plenty of opportunity to appreciate the landscapes of India, through much clearer

THE 50 GREATEST TRAIN JOURNEYS

windows than those found in ordinary Indian Railways air-conditioned coaches. The scenes of rural life are replicated right across the country: herds of long-eared goats looked after by children too young for school; bullocks or camels hauling carts wait at level crossings, their heads and necks in a haughty posture as though expressing their disdain for such humble work; women emerge from lush green fields with bundles of grass perched on their heads, making for a cluster of rudimentary dwellings with discs of dung, painstakingly arranged in herringbone fashion to form a beehive-shaped pile, drying in the sun. Those up early can see cooking fires being lit as dawn breaks.

Any rail buffs among the guests will relish the visit to the Maharaja of Gwalior's 400-room Jai Vilas Palace. The fabulously wealthy Scindia family had their own railway, beginning with a railway around the palace grounds and growing into a three-line network totalling 399 kilometres (248 miles). The railway contravened the British intention of retaining powers of railway construction, but since Madho Rao Scindia, who succeeded in 1886, had developed a practical love of railways and things mechanical under his British tutor, J.W. Johnstone, they accepted it. The ultimate seal of approval was given by the Viceroy, Lord Curzon, who opened the first two lines in 1899. H.F. Prevost Battersby, a British journalist accompanying the Prince of Wales during his 1903 visit, was amazed by Scindia's ability 'to drive car and locomotive or strip the works of either, as skilfully as a chauffeur or an engineer'. The Maharaja enjoyed driving the railway's second locomotive, a Kerr Stuart 4–4–0 built in Stoke-on-Trent, and it is said that it was fired on sandalwood and used jasmine oil for lubrication.

The Jai Vilas Palace was ready to receive Edward, Prince of Wales in 1875–6 during his 17-week tour of India. Even he must have been astonished by the Durbar Hall, lit by two 3.5-ton chandeliers – then the heaviest in the world – whose weight on the roof structure had caused such anxiety that it was tested by ten elephants using a specially built mile-and-a-quarter-long ramp. But Edward would not have seen one of the palace's most famous objects, the silver train carrying decanters and cigars around the long dining-table, which stops when a decanter or container is lifted; the train was supplied in 1906 by Armstrong Whitworth of Newcastle, with an override for the maharaja to omit a stop if he felt someone had had enough.

The final night is a concert of classical dance and buffet dinner, hosted by the Raja of Jehangirabad and his wife at their city palace in Lucknow, at which guests wear provided saris and kurta pyjamas. Then it's back to Delhi and service trains that can only leave something to be desired.

How long: 8 days

THE EASTERN & ORIENTAL EXPRESS (SINGAPORE–THAILAND)

This luxury emerald green and ivory train is imbued with a colonial-age ambience of rattan chairs on the veranda, linen suits and tea dances, reflecting the request made to the train's designer to base the interiors of the train on the 1932 film *Shanghai Express* which starred Marlene Dietrich. Operated by Belmond to its exacting standards, the train covers varied itineraries between Singapore, Malaysia, Thailand and Laos that last two to seven days.

The Classic Journeys are between Singapore and Bangkok,

covering 2,010 kilometres (1,249 miles), with less frequent alternatives that may entail a night at Raffles or the Cameron Highlands Resort. Knowledgeable guides give talks on the train as well as lead off-train excursions.

The train leaves from the relative quiet of Singapore's Woodlands station, where smartly uniformed attendants guide passengers to their small but beautifully formed compartments. Once across the Johor Causeway linking Singapore with Malaysia, the first of the gastronomic indulgences can begin. Life's pleasures don't get much better than enjoying good food, wine and conversation while pleasing landscapes glide past the window. White-flowered coffee trees and the pendulous pods of cocoa trees are novel sights to most European passengers, rather more attractive than the serried ranks of rubber trees in plantations beside the railway. Villages of stilted houses reached by ladder and surrounded by vegetable gardens, date palms and banana trees break up the commercial forests.

As the sun sets, heralding pre-prandial drinks, the train pauses at Kuala Lumpur's great white station building, completed in 1910 and combining elements of Moorish, Mughal and Saracenic architecture. The station now contains a small railway museum, since most trains now use Sentral station. The lights of the twin Petronas Towers stand out over the impressive skyline of Malaysia's capital, threaded by the elevated tracks of its excellent light rail transit system.

The open veranda of the Observation Car is perhaps best enjoyed around dawn, when the temperature is cooler and one can watch the mist rising from the forest. After breakfast and arrival at Butterworth, named after an early Straits Settlement governor, comes the first excursion, across the water to the island of Penang and a guided tour of George Town. This colonial settlement is now Malaysia's

second largest city, and part of its historic commercial centre was listed as a World Heritage Site in 2008. The tour takes in historic mosques, ornately roofed temples, churches and bazaars created in one of the first British trading centres in the East. Its best-known hotel, the E&O, was established in 1885 and gives its name to the train. It comes as no surprise to discover that its guests included Noël Coward, Rudyard Kipling and Somerset Maugham.

After rejoining the train for lunch, the passing landscape is still dotted with thatched houses on stilts, but vivid green rice paddies have replaced the forest. Ponderous water buffalo help straw-hatted farm workers as they wade through the paddies. Blink and you might miss the rapid costume change of the bar hostesses who reappear in Thai costumes and serve Thailand's Singha Gold beer instead of Singapore's Tiger brew. The transition from Muslim Malaysia to Buddhist Thailand is marked by a change from mosques to temples, the most elaborate having tiered roofs, decorative bargeboards and finials sculpted into serpentine shapes.

After breakfast on the third day, the E&O arrives at the River Kwai Bridge station, where the train stops for the final excursion. Guides escort guests on the short walk down to the jetty to board a local craft for a cruise along the lush greenery of the picturesque Kwai Yai River, passing under the famous bridge. It is not the original bridge of course; it isn't even the Kwai River and the bridge looks nothing like the wooden one in the film, which was shot in Sri Lanka. The 1957 film *The Bridge on the River Kwai* and the book on which it was based should have been called *The Bridge on the River Mae Khlung*. The author made an erroneous assumption. When large numbers of people came to see the bridge after watching the film, with consummate pragmatism the river was renamed the Kwai Yai (meaning 'Big Kwai').

E&O passengers are accompanied by a local historian who describes the history of the Thailand–Burma railway and the bridge. The visit includes the Thailand–Burma Railway Centre, with time to visit the Don Rak War Cemetery at Kanchanaburi, where 6,982 former prisoners of war are buried, mostly Australian, British and Dutch. Interest in the heartbreaking stories behind the railway has been fuelled by Eric Lomax's book *The Railway Man* and the film based on it starring Colin Firth and Nicole Kidman, and by Richard Flanagan's novel *The Narrow Road to the Deep North*, which won the 2014 Man Booker Prize.

After rejoining the train at Kanchanaburi railway station, lunch is served as the train rattles through the hinterland of Bangkok. The city draws closer and the press of urban life on the railway itself becomes almost alarming as the tracks cut a narrow swathe through the shanty towns and street markets, hawkers sometimes setting up their stall right beside the line. Bangkok's Hua Lamphong station is a contrast to the relative peace of Woodlands in Singapore; here the noise and bustle come as a shock after the serenity of the train, and passengers head off to find another calm oasis in their hotel.

How long: 4 days

TOKYO–NAGANO–YUDANAKA (JAPAN)

Shinkansen trains are synonymous with Japan, and this journey provides a contrast between the bullet train from Tokyo to Nagano and the kind of rural branch line that is

Photo: 663highland

a world away from the country's urban densities. The 3-foot 6-in (1,067-mm) gauge Nagano Electric Railway operates the 'Snow Monkey Express' to reach the hot-water pools known as 'onsen' near Yudanaka, where the famous snow monkeys (and humans) bathe while snow falls. There is even a Snow Monkey 1-Day Pass covering admission and travel from Nagano station.

It takes 90 minutes by the Asama Shinkansen from Tokyo to cover the 222 kilometres (138 miles) to Nagano in central Honshu (Japan's main island). High hills are almost constantly in view, many densely wooded. Nagano is itself worth a visit as an old cultural centre and the host of the 1988 Winter Olympics. The 7th-century Zenkōji Temple is within walking distance of the station and the magnificent Matsumoto Castle is a bus ride from the station. To the west lie the Japanese Alps, with mountains up to 3,000 metres (9,843 feet).

Yudanaka is reached by electric trains, and the hourly express is operated by units with the driver in an elevated cab like the Golden Panoramic Express in Switzerland. This gives a few lucky passengers the chance to sit at the front as the train begins its underground journey, with several sub-surface stations, before emerging to parallel a chain of hills, passing through orchards and small towns.

A bus from Yudanaka takes visitors to the foot of a 1.6-kilometre (1-mile) path with many steps, so suitable footwear with good grip is necessary. The 'Snow Monkeys' are Japanese macaques, with red faces and light brown fur. Touching them is strictly forbidden, but they are so accustomed to admiration that they have no hesitation in coming close to visitors.

How long: 3 hours

ALISHAN FOREST RAILWAY (TAIWAN)

Watching the sun rise over a sea of cloud that turns through every hue of pink encourages many visitors and Taiwanese to take one of the most bizarre railways in South-east Asia. The railway to the viewing platform at Zhushan in the Alishan Mountains is part of an 86-kilometre (53-mile) network of 2-foot 6-inch (762-mm) gauge railways that winds through the exceptionally precipitate mountains. Built while Formosa was under Japanese rule, the technical challenges were reflected in the construction time: begun in 1899, it was not opened until 1912.

Built to log Taiwan's central forests, this extraordinary railway ascends at fearsome gradients to the mountain resort of Alishan. Landslides sometimes disrupt services, but the journey is as much of an attraction as the destination. It climbs up the steep hillsides by a series of zig-zags, weaves through 50 tunnels and crosses 77 wooden bridges, ascending from tropical, through subtropical to temperate forest. It passes through agricultural land growing pineapples, mangoes, kiwi fruit, papayas, grapefruit, tobacco, bananas and betel palms, brightened by bursts of bougainvillea.

To cope with gradients as steep as 6.25 per cent (1 in 16), the railway used 20 Shay steam locomotives – geared machines designed by Ohio-born Ephraim Shay for use on poorly laid logging railways in mountain terrain. Higher up, the railway passes oolong tea plantations and orchards of cherries and plums.

In such difficult country, the railway has had its share of tribulations, with land movements causing derailments and a few serious accidents. However, the appeal of the railway has encouraged its reconstruction after major typhoon damage

Photo: maviscwling

in 2009, and it has been reopened. Diesel locomotives are used for most trains, but a number of Shay locomotives have been retained.

How long: 3 hours 15 minutes

AUSTRALASIA

THE GHAN (ADELAIDE–DARWIN)

Places that threaten survival have a certain mystique, and few more so than the Red Centre of Australia, which Jan Morris found 'more terrible by far than the Sahara or Empty Quarter'. Its epicentre is Alice Springs, which was already somewhere in the middle of nowhere when the railway arrived in 1929, thanks to an erratic waterhole, the Todd River and a repeater station on the Overland Telegraph line between Port Augusta and Darwin. The wire had gone live in 1872 with the message announcing that the station's intended first incumbent had died of thirst trying to get there.

Many farmers still had the delusion that South Australia could rival California in wheat production when a north–south railway to Darwin was talked of in the second half of the 19th century. In the event, it was cattle that sustained Alice, as it became known, with ranches the size of Belgium. That is, until it became a magnet for tourists wanting to see the largest monolith in the world, Ayer's Rock, or Uluru as it is called today.

The old narrow-gauge railway was so slow, curvaceous

and prone to flash floods that a new standard-gauge line was opened in 1980 and finally driven on to Darwin in 2004. Termites dining off the wooden sleepers didn't do much for the strength of the track, and derailments on the old line were not uncommon. One night in June 1954 almost every wheelset on the Ghan derailed, so the driver built a fire from scrub and dead branches for the passengers, knowing they would have a long wait for rescue. A passenger came up to him and asked whether he would like a beer. 'No thanks,' he replied, 'but I could do with a brandy.'

The train that has come to rival the Indian Pacific for the custom of visitors takes its name from the Afghans who came with camels imported from Karachi and Bombay to cope with the conditions of so much of Australia. The train is almost identical to the Indian Pacific, and Great Southern Railway has extended the schedule to allow more and longer off-train excursions.

The journey begins at Adelaide's modern station, a few kilometres from the city centre, and the train is soon bowling across the farming country of the Adelaide Plains with the 700-kilometre-long (435-mile) Flinders Ranges coming into view to the north. By Crystal Brook, sheep have been added to wheat. Unlovely Port Pirie is the centre of South Australia's heavy industry with colossal silver, lead and zinc smelters dominating the landscape. Within living memory, Port Pirie was notorious as the meeting point of three different track gauges, necessitating much changing and transhipment.

The estuary-like Spencer Gulf is within view for much of the way to Port Augusta, gateway to the outback and its vital supply centre. This was the southern terminus of the original narrow-gauge Ghan train, which began its slow and fitful service to Stuart – later renamed Alice Springs – in 1929. The Pichi Richi Railway track along the old route

Photo: Bahnfreund

of the Ghan can be seen heading off to the east on the 39 kilometres (24 miles) to Quorn, over which it operates a heritage steam-worked service. Port Augusta is an attractive town with single-storey houses in brick and stone surrounded by generous verandas.

It will almost certainly be dark as the train winds through sand hills and scrub forest before calling at Tarcoola in the small hours. If you are awake, it is worth getting off the train to be astounded by the brilliance of the night sky, so different from the northern hemisphere. Manguri is the stop for opal-rich Coober Pedy, where temperatures that can exceed 50°C have forced many inhabitants to live underground. There is even a Serbian underground church. A stop is made at Manguri for passengers to visit Coober Pedy and the mines that produce 70 per cent of the world's opals.

North of Kulgera is the Iron Man sculpture to comm-emorate the millionth track sleeper and the workers who laid them and built the line during the 1970s. As the train rumbles over the 15-span Finke River bridge, it is roughly as close as the railway gets to Uluru. The approach to Alice is unmistakeable. Ahead lie the tall MacDonnell Ranges, and the train heads for a gap so narrow that there is room only for the railway, the Todd River and a two-lane road. From a distance it looks as though a giant angle-grinder has been taken to the mountains.

Alice is like no other town, with its minority aboriginal population, its role as a hub for thousands of square miles around and as a tourist centre. Hemmed in by the surrounding hills, it is having to expand to the south beyond the MacDonnells. The railway made Alice: pastoralists could send livestock to Adelaide in days rather than months, and in the first ten months of railway service, 15,000 head of cattle worth $436,000 were railed south. The first train load of conducted tourists arrived in 1930. Today the Ghan stops long enough for a flight 416 kilometres (258 miles) to the south east to Uluru or tours of the town, variously visiting the Flying Doctor Service Museum, Anzac Hill, the Women Pioneers' hall of fame, a reptile centre and the wonderfully atmospheric Telegraph Station outside the town.

Pressing north across endless vistas of red earth under a sky of cobalt, the Ghan pauses at Tennant Creek, a centre of gold production and cattle stations of Santa Gertrudis and Brahman cattle. A longer stop is made at Katherine for a boat ride between the towering limestone walls of the crocodile-populated Nitmiluk Gorge, where the waters can rise 8 metres (26 feet) overnight. The first Australian feature film shot in colour, *Jedda* in 1955, was partly filmed in the gorge.

Katherine and the next station north, Pine Creek, had been on the railway before the Darwin line was opened; the narrow-gauge North Australia Railway operated a 509-kilometre (316-mile) line from Darwin through the two towns to Birdum, its weekly mixed train rising to 247 trains a week during the Second World War. It closed in 1976, but one of its locomotives, built in 1877 by Beyer, Peacock & Co. in Manchester, has been restored to working order and is displayed at the Pine Creek National Trust Museum.

The final stretch to Darwin is through densely forested country interspersed with mango plantations and watermelons before mangroves lining the Elizabeth River herald arrival in Darwin, Australia's only tropical city. There could hardly be a greater contrast between the glossy laurel-like leaves and white flowers of frangipanis typical of the city's luxuriant vegetation and the arid country through which the Ghan has passed for much of the journey.

How long: 2¼ days

ZIG ZAG RAILWAY (BLUE MOUNTAINS, NSW)

On 17 October 2013 fire swept through the western slopes of the Blue Mountains around Lithgow in New South Wales. It dealt probably the most savage blow to a heritage railway anywhere, destroying carriages, a railmotor, offices and workshop, spares and all services to the depot and station of the Zig Zag Railway.

Though only 7 kilometres (4.3 miles) long, this remarkable heritage railway covers what used to be a section of the main line linking Sydney and the prosperous farming areas and mineral deposits on the other side of the Blue Mountains. The zig-zag was the method chosen by John Whitton, Chief Engineer to the New South Wales Government Railways, who was charged with building the line, being cheaper than horseshoe curves and spirals.

The railway was badly needed. The roads were so bad that a bullock cart through the hills could manage no more than three or four miles a day. There was so much interest in the railway that it became a weekend excursion for Sydneyites to check progress. The Governor's wife, the Countess of Belmore, detonated an explosion to remove 45,000 tons of rock.

Around 700 workers toiled for 2½ years to build the railway, living in tents at 20 different locations with only two buildings, a bakery and the gunpowder store, despite winter temperatures as low as −10°C. Although a shelf was created along the contours wherever possible, Whitton still had to build one five-span and two eight-span viaducts and two tunnels to negotiate the ravines.

The zig-zag section of railway was opened without formal ceremony on 18 October 1869 and began its 41 years of linking Sydney with the interior, helping to develop western

Photo: Rangasyd

New South Wales. By the end of the 19th century, rail traffic over the Blue Mountains was so heavy that the single-track zig-zags had become a major bottleneck. A ten-tunnel deviation was built in 1907–10 and the old line was closed, the track lifted and the bush took over.

In 1969 negotiations began to restore the railway to working order, and in order to use locomotives and rolling stock from Queensland and South Australia, it was built to 3-foot 6-inch (1,067-mm) gauge rather than standard gauge. It reopened in stages between 1975 and 1988, and is one of very few heritage railways based on the importance of its civil engineering as well as the magnificent views over the densely forested slopes.

Its revival after the fire still hangs in doubt. It would be a great loss to railway history and Australia's Blue Mountain tourist industry if it is allowed to fail.

How long: 1 hour 30 minutes

THE INDIAN PACIFIC (SYDNEY–PERTH)

Few countries can offer a single rail journey from coast to coast and none as long as the Indian Pacific between Perth and Sydney, which takes about 72 hours to cover 4,352 kilometres (2,704 miles). A minority of passengers use it as transport, but the majority are tourists wanting to experience the extremes of Australia's varied terrain without the danger of driving.

The railway to link Western Australia with the east had been promised to encourage it to join the other colonies when they federated in 1900, in just the same way that British Columbia was persuaded to join Canada by the commitment to build a transcontinental railway. But it took a while, and the final link in the chain between Port Augusta and Kalgoorlie was not completed until 1917.

Even the 1908 surveying parties for the railway across arid Western Australia were a major challenge. One from Kalgoorlie entailed the use of 91 camels carrying 18 tons of supplies, creating water stations every seven miles and using a heavy chain dragged by camels to mark the trail. It took three months to chart 728 kilometres (452 miles) and meet the surveying party moving west from Port Augusta, which surveyed 972 kilometres (604 miles).

The first Indian Pacific didn't – in fact, couldn't – run much before its inauguration on 23 February 1970. The reason was the way the country's colonists ignored the advice of Earl Grey, the Secretary of State for the Colonies, who recommended in 1848 that standard gauge be adopted throughout Australia. Instead they established a world record for a single country by adopting 22 different track gauges. This lack of prescience was behind Mark Twain losing his rag at Albury in New South Wales while on a lecture tour in 1895, when he was turfed out of his train in the middle of the night because of the break of gauge at the border with Victoria. Twain and thousands like him over the centuries have fumed at the inconvenience and disrupted sleep.

Until 1937 a journey between Perth and Sydney required six changes of train, but decades of gauge conversion works finally created a unified track gauge from coast to coast. The Indian Pacific comprises stainless-steel lounge/bar and dining cars and sleeping cars offering Gold and Platinum Service. Both have private cabins with en-suite showers, but

Platinum is almost twice the size of Gold, with posher fittings and the option of breakfast in your cabin.

The Indian Pacific departs from Perth East station, where the waiting area has some fine railway memorabilia, including one of the first two coaches imported to Western Australia, in 1876, having been built at Saltley in Birmingham. As the train eases through the suburbs, it parallels the 3-foot 6-inch (1,067 mm) gauge tracks that make up much of Perth's commuter network. The line twists through the Avon Valley, the trees often brightened by parrots or black cockatoos.

The hills of the Darling ranges dwarf the line as the first lunch is served. The menu reflects the region being passed through, with such dishes as saltwater barramundi and grilled kangaroo fillet. The train ploughs across the wheatfields that provide Western Australia's breadbasket and passes the rail-served cereal silos of Merredin.

The first stop is at Kalgoorlie, where more gold has been won than anywhere else on earth. Within a week of its discovery in 1893, there were 1,400 prospectors in town. An off-train excursion takes passengers to the country's biggest open mine pit, and the town still has numerous historic buildings such as the magnificent towered post office. Eastwards, the country is so empty that the next hotel is 1,277 kilometres (793 miles) away at Tarcoola.

Perhaps the most unforgettable section of the Indian Pacific is the crossing of the Nullarbor Plain, the world's largest limestone karst landscape traversed by the longest stretch of dead straight railway track in the world, at 478 kilometres (297 miles). The change is sudden: 267 kilometres east of Kalgoorlie, the granite that has featured in outcrops dips below limestone, and the eucalyptus trees end. Nullarbor in Latin means 'no trees', but it is far from empty of life; you would be unlucky not to see camels, kangaroos or emus, and 794 species of plants and 56 species of mammals have been found within its expanse of 200,000 square kilometres (77,220 square miles).

The Nullarbor was dotted with tiny railway communities until wood sleepers were replaced by concrete, ending the need for daily inspection of the line by a ganger on foot. The communities were supplied by weekly 'tea and sugar trains', delivering all manner of supplies, but today only Father Christmas is taken out by the Great Southern Railway to communities on the Nullarbor. The country is so arid that the early explorers all grew beards; you wouldn't waste water for shaving in this country.

At Rawlinna the westbound train stops for a sunset dinner, while eastbound passengers are given an hour or so to explore the best-known of the communities at Cook, which has a fluctuating population but never more than a single digit. There isn't much to see: a row of houses, some derelict buildings and a few vehicles that haven't turned a wheel in decades, ancient 'his' and 'hers' holding cells near the platform and a shop in the station building. But the atmosphere leaves a deep impression; most depart wondering how they would cope with such profound isolation – and feeling profoundly grateful they don't have to.

At the end of the Nullarbor the railway enters an area of sandhills, the vegetation gradually thickening, though the Nullarbor morphs into the fringe of the Great Victoria Desert. Tarcoola is the junction for the 'new' line to Alice Springs, which opened in 1980, and the 2004 extension to Darwin (see page 178). The Indian Pacific continues past market gardens and the junction for Sydney at Crystal Brook and continues on to reach Adelaide.

Many choose to break the journey here, either to take the Ghan to Darwin or to get to know the fascinating planned

Photo: Bahnfreund

city named after William IV's wife. Its ideal of 'a quarter acre block for all' and landscaped streets and parks, best appreciated in North Adelaide, was the inspiration for Britain's Ebenezer Howard and the garden city movement. The westbound Indian Pacific offers a stop in Adelaide long enough for an immersive tour of the wine-producing Barossa region and a tour of the city with a 'dining experience' at the National Wine Centre.

Retracing its steps to Crystal Brook but turning east, the Indian Pacific glides through the wheatfields of South Australia and Gladstone, where a break of gauge once gave rise to a two-storey station with refreshment rooms and a hotel. At Jamestown, passengers may get a glimpse of the fine station, which is now a museum looked after by the National Trust, but it is the Steam Heritage Rail Centre at Peterborough that excites rail buffs – its roundhouse depot has what is claimed to be the world's only turntable with three track gauges.

In Peterborough's main street is a statue of 'Bob, the railway dog', a German Coolie/Smithfield cross who loved riding on the footplate of steam locomotives and was well known to enginemen throughout South Australia. He wore a stout collar with a brass plate inscribed, 'Stop me not, but let me jog, For I am Bob, the drivers dog', which is now in the National Railway Museum in Adelaide.

Around Cockburn, the symbol of the Indian Pacific, the wedge-tailed eagle and the country's largest eagle, may be seen riding the currents. A long stop is made at Broken Hill, made rich from 1883 by a long lode of silver, zinc and lead, which paid for the impressive public buildings that encourage some to break their journey here. Besides underground mine tours, the town has a restored mosque built for Afghan camel drivers, art galleries and a transport museum.

The town of Menindee floats among undulating red sand dunes near the Menindee Lakes system, which holds more water than Sydney Harbour. Kangaroos and emus can often be seen from the train. Near Orange, named after the Prince, is the highest feature between Perth and Sydney, Mount Canobolas, an extinct volcano reaching 1,395 metres (4,577 feet).

The railway twists and turns down a steep incline to reach the agricultural centre of Bathurst, the oldest settlement west of the Great Dividing Range, which offers walking tours of its historic buildings. The last stop before Sydney is Lithgow, starting point of the heritage Zig Zag Railway, which has preserved one of the Victorian civil engineering wonders of the country, but suffered a devastating fire in 2013 and had to suspend operations. Its viaducts and different levels can be seen from the Indian Pacific as it leaves for the stiff climb up to Katoomba at 1,000 metres (3,281 feet) above Sydney in the Blue Mountains.

Impenetrable bush, eucalyptus and ironbark forest and sheer rock faces deterred exploration of these mountains until the drought of 1813 forced colonists inland. Katoomba is a popular resort for visitors and served by express and suburban services from Sydney. Among the attractions is what is claimed to be the world's steepest funicular railway, the Katoomba Scenic Railway, with a gradient of 1 in 0.78. Travelling in glass-roofed carriages, passengers on the scenic railway travel through a cliff-side tunnel and can take a 2.4-kilometre (1.5-mile) walk through rainforest.

The views leaving Katoomba are just as impressive: the Indian Pacific has to crawl round tight curves as it loses height to reach the coastal bowl near Penrith. Rubbing shoulders with commuter trains as it weaves through the suburbs, the Indian Pacific terminates beneath the overall roof at the great sandstone edifice of Sydney Central station, dominated by its 75-metre (246-foot) clock-tower, opened in 1906. It is a suitably grand ending to one of the world's longest train journeys.

How long: 3 days

TRANZALPINE (CHRISTCHURCH–GREYMOUTH)

One of KiwiRail's three scenic trains, the TranzAlpine, deserves its reputation as one of the world's great railway journeys, linking east-coast Christchurch with the west coast at Greymouth by a crossing of the Southern Alps – the 'northern' Alps are those in Europe. The 233-kilometre (145-mile) journey attracts large numbers of passengers ashore from the cruise terminal at Lyttelton as well as travellers touring New Zealand. An observation car allows easy photography of the landscapes where the *Lord of the Rings* films were shot.

Though Christchurch's 1950s-built second station and clock tower was a casualty of the 2010–11 earthquakes, it had already been replaced in 1993 by a third station designed largely for tourist traffic. The TranzAlpine begins its journey by crossing New Zealand's most fertile granary, the 777,000 hectares (1,920,008 acres) of Canterbury Plains; it's the country's largest area of flat land and produces more than 90 per cent of its milling wheat.

Billiard-table fields of cereals and cattle are sheltered by lines of columnar trees against the cold southerly and north-westerly winds. Springfield was the start of the climb into the Alps, and over 70 railwaymen were once based here at the locomotive depot. Huge K^B 4-8-4 locomotives, with the largest grate area of any 3-foot 6-inch (1,067-mm) gauge locomotives in the world, came on here for the slog ahead into the snow-covered mountains.

For much of the way to the summit at Arthur's Pass, the line parallels the Waimakariri River with spectacular views into a deepening sheer-faced gorge between sixteen tunnels. The highest of five viaducts at 73 metres (240 feet) is the Staircase Viaduct, built by the Cleveland Bridge & Engineering Company of Darlington in 1908. The country is desolate with barely a sign of habitation among the marshes and fields beside the river, which broadens into a straggling mass of braided channels as the valley widens.

The lonely country was captured in a 1936 canvas by Rita Angus of Cass station, which hangs in Christchurch Art Gallery and was voted New Zealand's favourite painting in 2006. Even today, the site of the station has only a few neighbouring homesteads and a university field station set up in 1914 to study alpine flora and habitats.

The small settlement of Arthur's Pass is the highest on the South Island, at 737 metres (2,418 feet), and a stop is made here for passengers to stretch their legs and take in the surrounding beech-forested peaks. The first party of Europeans to cross the pass, in 1864, was led by Islington-born (later Sir) Arthur Dobson, who had been commissioned to find a route across the mountains to the newly discovered west-coast goldfields.

The 8.5-kilometre (5.3-mile) Otira Tunnel just south of Arthur's Pass station was the most difficult and costly construction on the railway, begun in 1886 and opened only in August 1923. During the First World War, Otira tunnellers were sent to the Western Front to mine under the enemy

Photo: Johannes Vogel

trenches. Because the gradient falls towards the west coast at 1 in 33, electric traction was used from the start, but in 1997 the ageing catenary was decommissioned and diesel traction took over. Tunnel doors and fans were installed to expel the pollution.

Until 1923 passengers were transferred to Cobb & Co. horse-drawn coaches licensed to carry fourteen passengers and mail, and it was often an exhilarating and wet experience – Arthur's Pass receives 424 centimetres (167 inches) of rain a year.

On the west side of Otira Tunnel is the railway colony of Otira, where 200 railwaymen once lived in houses provided by the railway. The canny local policeman once identified the culprit stealing locomotive coal by placing small cracker explosives in the coal pile.

The TranzAlpine joins the Grey River, named after George Grey, the country's longest-serving Governor to whom there's a memorial in the crypt of St Paul's Cathedral. The coastal plain is flat and covered by peat bogs, red pine, flax and crack willow. Only cattle are seen hereabouts as the west coast is too wet for sheep, and dairy farming has generated enough traffic for milk trains. There are sawmills and relics of the coal-mining that sustained the area's communities, populated by miners who emigrated from the Durham and Scottish coalfields in the 19th century.

The train skirts Lake Brunner, famous for trout fishing, and pauses at Moana station, which is the finest remaining example of a Class A station designed by Sir George Troup, who was the first official architect to New Zealand Railways and designed the magnificent station at Dunedin. Stationmasters were often also the postmaster in smaller settlements.

A large number of yachts heralds arrival at Greymouth, where many passengers begin journeys along the west coast;

others repair to the old harbour offices, which are now a restaurant and microbrewery with vast gleaming copper vat. However, it's well worth making the return journey: the sun has swung round, presenting a quite different picture of some of the South Island's finest scenery.

How long: 4 hours 30 minutes

THE AMERICAS

THE CANADIAN (TORONTO–VANCOUVER)

This epic journey between Toronto and Vancouver is the flagship train of VIA, which operates Canada's remaining longer-distance passenger services. Along with the Trans-Siberian, it is on many a 'must-do' travel list, not only for the landscapes and pleasure of being on a comfortable and relaxing journey, but also for the idea of crossing such a vast country. Of course, that's not strictly true in the way that Australia's Indian Pacific is a coast-to-coast journey; to do that in Canada, one would need to begin in Halifax, but the Canadian is still a 3½-day journey covering 4,466 kilometres (2,775 miles).

It's a route redolent with history, even though some settlements on the way are barely a century old. Canada might not exist in the same way geopolitically if it wasn't for the railway: it was the promise of a transcontinental railway that persuaded British Columbia to join the Canadian Confederation rather than entertain overtures from the United States. Though the Canadian between Toronto and Vancouver travels over the tracks of the second transcontinental railway, the Canadian National, the experience makes it easy to understand why the iron road and its colourful history is woven into the Canadian DNA.

The Canadian was inaugurated in 1955 using a new train of streamlined stainless-steel coaches. The same coaches operate the train today, following periodic refurbishments to improve their amenities. There are sleeping cars with en-suite showers, dining cars and lounge cars with vistadomes for panoramic views, and there are film screenings, wine tastings and talks on subjects such as the country's maritime history or First Nations' culture. In high season this village on wheels is so long that the staff cleaning the windows at Jasper wear rollerblades to whip up and down the train.

For those who love history and want a deeper understanding of the terrain and places, there are mile-by-mile guides identifying passing rivers, lakes and mountains; giving the story behind such buildings as the engine house at Hornepayne, Ontario, where its turntable had to be covered because of the volume of snowfall each winter; or on the origin of place names – for example, that Jasper takes its name from Jasper Hawes, who founded the North West Company trading post in 1817. Readers learn that Biggar was named after the solicitor for the Grand Trunk Pacific Railway, and that its slogan 'New York is big, but this is Biggar' dates from the founding of the town and railway division point in 1909. They also warn of the approach of a good photographic opportunity.

The Canadian's departure station is a suitably grand affair for a transcontinental journey; Toronto's Union station is Canada's finest Beaux-Arts station, and its immense departure hall prepares you for something impressive.

Built in 1915–20, the hall's cornice contains a roll-call of destinations across the country, heralding some of the places en route.

As the train eases out of Union station, there's a grandstand view over Lake Ontario and the famous CN Tower. Beneath it is the old 32-stall locomotive roundhouse, now home to the Steam Whistle micro-brewery and the Toronto Railway Museum. The museum's showpiece is the huge Canadian National 4-8-4 No. 6213, and it has a collection of rolling stock and a simulator offering the chance to drive over Toronto's tracks in the 1950s.

Once Toronto is left behind, there's a day traversing the rocks, lakes and boreal forest of the vast Canadian Shield that almost rings Hudson Bay. British ancestry is obvious from the names of many settlements on the journey and even from the waterways – the train criss-crosses the Trent-Severn Canal/Waterway before reaching the distinctive landscape of the Canadian Shield. Covering over half of Canada, the Shield's thin soil supports dense boreal forest broken up by bare rock, rivers and a multitude of lakes. It's a measure of the scale of Canada that the train passes a game reserve of 7,000 square kilometres (2,703 square miles) at Chapleau, the largest in the world. Moose, deer, mountain goats and even bears can be glimpsed during the journey. The occasional sight of a smelter reminds one of the mineral riches buried beneath the Shield, and station museums and even plinthed steam locomotives and cabooses on platforms testify to the role of the railway in forging Canada as a country.

As spruce trees give way to the flat prairie of Manitoba, the sky and distant horizon assume a greater importance. In autumn that sky can be filled with formations of waterfowl in unimaginable numbers. There are so many lakes in the

Photo: Timothy Stevens

section east of Winnipeg that the Canadian National Railway encouraged the construction of lakeside weekend cottages and ran special Friday and Sunday evening trains to link them with the provincial capital.

After so much emptiness, it almost comes as a shock to see the Winnipeg skyline. The hour or so pause here gives time to admire the magnificent station designed by the same architects as New York's Grand Central station. Its Rotunda is so fine that it was used as the setting for concerts and even decorated with streamers and lanterns for the city's New Year's Ball. There is plenty of time to stretch one's legs during the four-hour eastbound stop, perhaps wandering to the Forks market in the restored warehouses beside the confluence of the Red and Assiniboine rivers, where traders have met for millennia.

Anyone who thinks the prairies are flat and uninteresting is in for a pleasant surprise as the Canadian returns to farmland. The railway has to leap across valleys on tall, long trestle viaducts – Saskatoon is known as the 'City of Bridges' – and potatoes and sunflowers intersperse pasture and the more frequent crop of wheat. Gazing out at the fertile landscape, it's hard to imagine what it must have been like for early settlers little more than a century ago to arrive at their quarter-section to make a new life with nothing more than the tools, seeds and belongings they could carry. The occasional sighting of the silver dome of a Ukrainian or Eastern Orthodox church testifies to the distances some of them had travelled to find a new home.

Lakes fill bowls among the hills of large cattle ranches as the train heads into oil-bearing strata beyond Chauvin, marked by the bizarre nodding donkeys, or pumpjacks, dotting the ground. They herald the oil refineries of Edmonton, Alberta's provincial capital, and a stopping-off point for travellers visiting, among the city's attractions, Canada's largest open-air museum at Fort Edmonton Park, with its own full-size steam and electric railway.

Past Hinton it's wise to take a seat in the dome car before the Miette Range announces the approach to the Rockies and mountain landscapes on a monumental scale. The railway crosses on a long viaduct the 1,224-kilometre-long (761-mile) Athabasca River, renowned for its turquoise colour, before entering Jasper National Park. A stop at Jasper is long enough for passengers to visit the shops along nearby Connaught Drive and admire the behemoth that used to haul trains like the Canadian – the Mountain U-1-a steam locomotive of 1923, which has been on its plinth at Jasper station since 1972. When you get back on board you'll find the windows of the train have been cleaned for the sights ahead.

Soon after passing Yellowhead Lake, Mount Robson (3,954 metres/12,972 feet), the tallest mountain in the Canadian Rockies, comes into view just across the border in British Columbia. The mountain is so large that it has its own microclimate. A succession of majestic sights follow: Pyramid Falls; the North Thompson, Thunder and Blue river crossings; Kamloops Lake; Rainbow Canyon and its multi-coloured rock faces; and one of the most spectacular stretches of the whole journey, through the Fraser River canyon past Hell's Gate, named by the explorer Simon Fraser because it was a place 'where no human should venture'. The train gingerly picks its way along a shelf above the V-shaped gorge, with a cablecar above and a fish ladder below to help spawning salmon battle upstream.

As the gorge widens at Yale, there is a huge black rock in the middle of the river, which was named after Lady Franklin following her visit in 1861, 14 years after the death of her husband while searching for the North West Passage. The hills shrink and end as rugged country gives way to forest and then lush market gardens thriving on the silt washed down by the Fraser River over thousands of years. Many of the ingredients in the menus of Vancouver's renowned restaurants come from this area.

The replica of the Hudson Bay Company's large post at Fort Langley can be seen from the train, and journey's end is close when the Canadian clatters across New Westminster Bridge, built in 1904 with an opening span for Fraser River shipping. A suitably grand station, the Pacific Central edifice of 1919 welcomes passengers arriving in British Columbia's largest city, where the Fairmont Hotel Vancouver has been receiving rail-borne guests since it was opened by the Canadian Pacific Railway in 1939, just in time to receive George VI and Queen Elizabeth. Few cities could match the scenic delights along the route of the Canadian, but Vancouver does, with its glorious position overlooking the sea and the North Shore Mountains.

How long: 3½ days

ALASKA RAILROAD (ANCHORAGE–FAIRBANKS)

The Alaska Railroad is like no other United States railway. It is state-owned though operated as a private business and was one of the last US railroads to be built, opened on 15 July 1923 by President Warren Harding, who died a fortnight later from food poisoning contracted on his way back to San Francisco.

Today various seasonally timetabled trains are operated over all or part of the 747-kilometre (464-mile) main line between Seward, Anchorage and Fairbanks. The remoteness of the country is reflected in operation of one of the last flagstop trains in North America; passengers can get off the train wherever they please and flag it down to board on the 88-kilometre (55-mile) journey of the Hurricane Turn train north of Talkeetna.

The train used by most tourists is the flagship Denali Star between Anchorage and Fairbanks, which relies heavily on cruise-ship passengers. The consist includes double-deck dome cars with an upper-level outdoor viewing deck and a lower-level dining room, but the coaches vary between the cruise companies, which own their own stock, as well as those owned by the Alaska Railroad. The journey takes twelve hours and the cruise companies all break the journey at Denali National Park and/or Talkeetna, so to do it in a single day you have to travel in the Alaska Railroad coaches.

Leaving the headquarters of the railroad at Anchorage, the Denali Star scythes through the suburbs of Alaska's largest city, which suffered the second largest earthquake in recorded history, at 9.2, in 1964. It left few old buildings. Birch forests surround the Eagle and Chugiak rivers, leading to a watershed that's home to moose and bears.

Before Talkeetna is reached there are views of the tallest mountain in North America: Denali was known as Mount McKinley, after the 25th President of the USA, until approval was given to its renaming by President Obama in August 2015. The 6,190-metre-high (20,308-foot) mountain was first climbed in 1913 and has five glaciers flowing off its slopes.

The Denali Star stops at the former gold-mining town of Talkeetna, but then almost any settlement in the state has historic links with gold. The Talkeetna Mountains tower above the railway as it follows the twists of the Susitna River,

Photo: Nils Öberg

frequented by black and brown bears. Beaver may be spotted in Indian River Canyon as the train climbs to the tree line and crosses the bridge with the longest span on the line at 279 metres (915 feet), over Hurricane Gulch, and the highest, 90 metres (296 feet) above the water.

The train climbs towards Broad Pass, the highest point on the line at 720 metres (2,363 feet), with some of the best views of the journey over lakes and snow-dappled mountains. Shortly before Denali Park station, the train crosses Riley Creek trestle. Its steelwork was made in Pennsylvania and shipped through the Panama Canal to be loaded on to 24 rail cars for the journey to the site. Assembly took place during January 1922, despite sub-zero temperatures and limited hours of daylight. A steam crane crossed the bridge in less than a month.

Many passengers opt to spend a night or two in Denali National Park to admire the mountain and to see moose, bears, wolves, Dall sheep and the caribou that migrate through the area in the autumn. The railway drops down through the fearsome, steep-sided canyon of the Nenana River; passengers often see whitewater rafting expeditions struggling through the difficult waters. After the coal-mining town of Healy, the train reaches Clear Site and its nearby US Air Force station.

Now housing a museum, Nenana station dates from 1922 and is on the National Register of Historic Places. The station hosted President Warren Harding in 1923 when he came to drive in the golden spike at the end of the Mears Memorial Bridge over the Tanana River. Named after Col. Frederick Mears, the railroad's builder, the through-truss bridge has a 210-metre (689-foot) span, still the longest in Alaska.

After passing the station, the train describes a horseshoe bend to climb on to the bridge and continue north through boreal forest of aspen, birch and willow broken by areas of marsh. An occasional hunting village and crossing of the Parks Highway are the only signs of civilisation as the train reaches the 'Land of the Midnight Sun' above ground, and permafrost below.

Arrival in Fairbanks is heralded by the University of Alaska, followed by railroad yards. Alaska's second largest city attracts visitors for the Northern Lights and The World Ice Art Championships.

How long: 12 hours

ROCKY MOUNTAINEER (VANCOUVER–JASPER/ BANFF/SEATTLE)

Sir William Cornelius Van Horne would have been delighted by the success of Rocky Mountaineer. As President of the Canadian Pacific Railway (CPR), Van Horne did more than any other individual to promote the spectacular landscapes of the Canadian Rockies and the train as the best way to enjoy them. Since services began in 1990, over 2 million people have travelled on Rocky Mountaineer's trains, which have earned the company numerous awards.

Few knew much about the Canadian Rockies when the first transcontinental train made what was then the world's longest railway journey, arriving in Vancouver on 23 May 1887 from Montreal after 4,665 kilometres (2,899 miles). Van Horne encouraged artists and photographers to capture the natural beauty of the vast area, also visited by the conqueror of the Matterhorn, Edward Whymper, who coined the catch-phrase 'fifty Switzerlands in one', which CPR used in its promotions.

Rocky Mountaineer trains run in daylight hours so that passengers don't miss any of the scenery. The onboard hosts make sure you can be ready to photograph a waterfall or glacier and talk about the topography and the natural and human history of the places en route. Even the engineer on the locomotive alerts hosts to wildlife, and passengers often see moose, deer, coyote, elk, bears and eagles. Even beavers are sometimes spotted.

There are five routes to choose from, though Rocky Mountaineer offers over 45 different packages between April and October, some including a cruise north to Alaska or from Seattle, starting point for the most recently introduced Coastal Passage train service, which is full of contrasts. Once Vancouver and the immense bridges over the Fraser River are left behind, the line passes heron-stalked creeks, ploughs through fields of blueberries and corn with distant mountains as a backcloth, and skirts the sea for mile after mile with bleached and stripped tree trunks littering the shore.

First-time visitors to the Rockies usually choose one of the two routes between Vancouver and either Jasper – Journey through the Clouds – or Banff – First Passage to the West. Both follow the same route from Vancouver as far as the overnight stop at Kamloops, where they diverge on the second day.

Leaving the Rocky Mountaineer's commodious station in Vancouver, there's time to familiarise yourself with the train and your fellow passengers before you reach Hope, where the Fraser and Coquihalla rivers meet and the scenery becomes an uninterrupted joy. At Yale the railway clings to the side of the V-shaped valley above the Fraser River and its narrowest point at Hell's Gate, named for obvious reasons by the explorer Simon Fraser.

At Lytton the clear waters of the Thompson River are sullied at the confluence with the muddy Fraser, and whitewater rafters are often seen battling the currents. Sagebrush and bunchgrass become the dominant vegetation in the arid country after Spences Bridge, the only rich greens flanking the river. The train skirts Kamloops Lake before arriving at the town and the bus waiting to take you to a hotel.

Journey through the Clouds follows the valley of the North Thompson River and through the gap between the Cariboo and Monashee mountains, passing such sights as the 91-metre (299-foot) drop of Pyramid Falls and the Albreda Glacier before joining the route of the Rainforest to Gold Rush train past Mount Robson to reach Jasper.

First Passage to the West leaves Kamloops alongside the South Thompson River which it follows to the tentacles of Shuswap Lake, ringed by mountains. The train rumbles past Craigellachie, named by Van Horne, where one of the most reproduced historic photographs was taken. Here, in 1885, the most senior director of the CPR, Donald A. Smith, hammered in the last spike of the Canadian Pacific, symbolising the tying together of the country.

The railway runs right beside the thunderous waters of the Illecillewaet River through the canyon after Revelstoke as the train climbs towards the Connaught Tunnel and a breathtaking panorama of mountains as it leaves the northern portal. Audible gasps through the carriage mark the crossing of the famous metal arch of Stoney Creek Bridge and the chasm beneath.

For many, the climax of the journey is the view as the train climbs partly through spiral tunnels in Mount Ogden and Cathedral Mountain to the Continental Divide at Stephen.

Photo: The Land

A stop at the station for Lake Louise, famed for its beauty and the railway-built hotel overlooking it, was introduced for those wanting to visit Château Lake Louise. But the descent to Banff with fabulous views over the turquoise Bow River in the soft clear light of a summer evening is no anti-climax.

The two-day Rainforest to Gold Rush train offers a very different experience from the two classic trains through the Rockies, though it too is seldom out of sight of mountains. It leaves from North Vancouver station and weaves a sinuous path in and out of the coves along Howe Sound. Breakfast is served as you gaze over the dark island-studded waters of the sound to the conifer-covered mountain slopes on the far shore of the fjord. The engineer obligingly slows for the passage of Cheakamus Canyon on a ledge above the churning waters, the open-sided car in the train filled with the sound of camera shutters.

Heading for the overnight stop in a hotel in the attractive Cariboo town of Quesnel, the train scythes through fields of fruit and vegetables around Pemberton before being dwarfed by the Cadwallader peaks to the west. Few stretches of railway beside water can rival the shoreline passage of Anderson and emerald-green Seton lakes, separated by an isthmus and portage so busy in goldrush days that it was nicknamed 'Wapping'.

After the end of Seton Lake, the mountains suddenly fall away as the valley meets the Fraser River, whose gold-lined sandbars lured thousands into the Cariboo. At Lillooet the train crosses the Fraser River, its water the colour of milk chocolate, and begins a long and spectacular climb out of the valley to reach a plateau of horse and cattle ranches. The curves are so sharp that the sound of treadles operating flange-lubricators beside the rails is frequently heard. At the top of the climb, the train bowls across a plateau of rolling hills, forest and clearings for beef cattle ranches. Huge tracts of land here were bought by English aristocrats, giving their names to some of the railway's stations, such as Exeter and Tatton.

After the night in Quesnel, the train continues north to Prince George where it turns south east along the Rocky Mountain Trench, the longest valley in North America. Tiny communities dependent on logging and smallholdings flash by, and station loops are often occupied by immense freight trains heading for the coast at Prince Rupert. Past Tête Jaune Cache, the highest mountain in the Canadian Rockies comes into view: Mount Robson at 3,954 metres (12,972 feet) can be admired for about ten miles. Its immense size – big enough to create a microclimate – is awe-inspiring. The train skirts crystal-clear Moose Lake, abundant source of rainbow trout, before reaching the Continental Divide near Yellowhead Pass and descending to journey's end at Jasper. Thankfully the landscapes have changed little from the time Van Horne wanted others to enjoy them.

How long: 4–16 days

COAST STARLIGHT (SEATTLE–LOS ANGELES)

For a romantic overnight journey, this takes some beating, with its unrivalled coastal views along Puget Sound and beside the Pacific. Perhaps that's why it often attracts a younger clientele than other long-distance Amtrak trains. The parlour cars have been refurbished, and there is even a cinema with 50-inch plasma monitors for after-dark movies as well as board games and a library. Daily wine tastings

Photo: Steve Wilson

complement the regional fare of dishes such as Pacific Bay scallops and Santa Maria beef short-ribs.

This 2,203-kilometre (1,369-mile) single-night journey along the Pacific coast begins at Seattle's magnificently restored King Street station of 1904–6, with its great domed hall and clock-tower modelled on the Campanile di San Marco in Venice. Another skyward construction, the Space Needle built for the 1962 World Fair, can be seen as the train rolls through the city and suburbs and past the Boeing Field test site where there is a Museum of Flight with a Concorde.

South of the port city of Tacoma and its wood-domed stadium, the coastal scenery is spectacular, with views across Puget Sound of the Olympic Mountains, while inland rises the volcanic peak of Mount St Helens. The train crosses numerous rivers finding their way to the sea and follows the Columbia River, which until the war of 1812 marked the border between Canada and the USA. Vancouver (USA) was the site of a Hudson's Bay Company fort built in 1824, making it the oldest continuous settlement in the Pacific Northwest. Today the Columbia River marks the state border between Washington and Oregon.

One of the US's greenest cities, Portland is a good place to break the journey, not least for its fine art museum and the ease of getting around by its light rail network and 512 kilometres (318 miles) of bike lanes and trails. Its vast brick station – the original plans were for something even bigger – was completed in 1896, and its 45.7-metre (150-foot) clock tower gives the sensible advice to 'Go by train' in neon signs put up in 1948.

Leaving Portland, the Coast Starlight threads the Willamette Valley, with the Cascades to the east and the Coast Range to the west. The varied landscapes range from soft-fruit farms and vineyards to sawmills before the train winds into the Cascade Mountains, clothed in Douglas firs and streaked with waterfalls. White pelicans may be seen in the vast Upper Klamath Lake as the train drops towards the Californian border with views of the highest peak, Mount Shasta, at 4,322 metres (14,180 feet).

Rail buffs may wish to pause in the state capital of Sacramento for the imaginative displays in the California State Railroad Museum, one of the world's great transport museums. Sacramento was where railroad construction began eastwards to meet up at Promontory Point in Utah. At Oakland, the railway picks up the route of El Camino Real, the Spanish mission road along which a chain of 21 missions was founded a day's horseback journey apart, built from 1769 to 1823.

After the notional capital of Silicon Valley at San Jose, the train moves from California's high-tech industries to more aesthetically pleasing sights along the Santa Clara Valley and fields of garlic, mushrooms, artichokes, lettuces, flowers and vines. The people who worked this land were evocatively portrayed by John Steinbeck, whose boyhood home in Salinas has been preserved.

Fertile farmland is followed by the Santa Cruz and San Benito mountains. The climb through the Cuesta Pass into the Santa Margarita Mountains is spectacular as the train describes great horseshoe curves to reach the palms of San Luis Obispo for Randolph Hearst's nearby castle. The journey concludes with mile after mile beside the ocean, enlivened by lighthouses, birdlife and surfers, and a final mountain section before Los Angeles.

The Coast Starlight draws to a halt at Union station, completed in 1939 in the Spanish Mission style that characterises southern California with touches of Art Deco. The station is served by three Metro rail lines and provides a connection to Amtrak's South West Chief to Chicago and the Sunset Limited to New Orleans.

How long: 36 hours

CALIFORNIA ZEPHYR (CHICAGO–SAN FRANCISCO)

Linking the Windy City and its celebrated modern architecture with the west coast, the daily two-night California Zephyr is Amtrak's longest route at 3,901 kilometres (2,424 miles). In spring and summer, National Park Service rangers give a commentary during the section through the canyons of the Rockies, but a winter journey has its appeal with snow on the mountains and razor-sharp light.

Thirteen Amtrak routes serve Chicago's Union station, which opened in 1925. Its Beaux-Arts limestone façades, Corinthian-columned front entrance and magnificent marble-floored hall lit by brass lamps make it one of the city's architectural highlights.

As the Zephyr leaves Union station, it brushes the south branch of the Chicago River, which had its direction of flow reversed in a major construction project of the 1890s, in order to improve the water quality of Lake Michigan. The extensive suburbs and industrial districts of Chicago are a good time to explore the train and find the dining-car and the Sightseer Lounge/café car with its panoramic-windowed lounge on the upper level and café below.

Aurora was dubbed 'City of Lights' for becoming the first US city to have electric lights, and its 1866-built stone roundhouse for locomotives was incorporated into a transportation centre on the north side of the line. The train heads across the flat, fertile farmland of central Illinois to reach Princeton, which claims to be 'the pig capital of the world'.

The railroad town of Galesburg celebrates its heritage at the Galesburg Railroad Museum and the National Railroad Hall of Fame, as well as with a Burlington Route Hudson locomotive plinthed by the station. Fields of corn and grazing cattle slowly morph into wetlands and woodland as the train crosses into Iowa and clatters across the Mississippi River at Burlington. The 654-metre (2,146-foot) steel bridge is the third railway bridge on the site, completed in 2011 with a vertical-lift truss span for taller vessels. Before the first bridge was finished in 1868, passengers crossed by ferry or on foot across the ice in winter. For rail buffs, Burlington was the birthplace in 1863 of the Westinghouse brake, a system adopted all over the world.

As the train passes Stanton, two bizarre water towers can be seen, shaped and painted to resemble a coffee pot and a coffee cup; they commemorate an actress in a coffee commercial who was born in the town. Besides being the start of the Mormon Trail, Council Bluffs was chosen by President Lincoln as the eastern end of the Union Pacific Railroad, which is recalled in the town's UP Railroad Museum. Adjacent to the Union Pacific's main yard is the 17-metre-high (56-foot) Golden Spike Monument of gold-coloured concrete, unveiled in 1939 to commemorate the 70th anniversary of the joining of Union Pacific and Central Pacific rails.

The Missouri River, marking the Iowa/Nebraska border, is crossed just east of Omaha on an 11-span truss bridge completed in 1916. Union Station in Omaha is an outstanding example of Art Deco. It was built in 1929–31 to the design of Los Angeles architect Gilbert Stanley Underwood, who is best known for his National Park lodges. The steel-framed structure has a cladding of cream-coloured glazed terracotta, and the Belgian-marbled Great Hall is lit by six immense chandeliers. The station also contains the oldest locomotive owned by Union Pacific, 4-6-0 No. 1243 of 1890, which is often referred to as the 'Harriman engine', since it is the only locomotive still owned by Union Pacific from the era when E.H. Harriman controlled the railroad. The museum also contains Abraham Lincoln's funeral car with original fittings.

Having crossed the Platte River, which the Mormons followed, the Zephyr arrives at Hastings, where 60 buildings in Railroad Town have been re-erected to re-create a late 19th-century prairie community. Arable farming gives way to cattle pasture as the train nears Colorado, and the country becomes visibly drier.

Gold brought the mile-high city of Denver into being, and the surviving sections of the narrow-gauge railroads built to serve mining operations have become major tourist attractions (see page 222). Marvellous views of the city follow departure as the line begins its spectacular climb into the Rockies, burrowing through 27 tunnels in 21 curvaceous kilometres (13 miles), the longest being the summit Moffat Tunnel at 10 kilometres (6 miles) and the highest point on Amtrak's network – 2,820 metres (9,252 feet). There are fine views over the Colorado plains on the climb, and ski lifts are visible from the train around Winter Park, where temperatures can dip to –46°C (–50°F).

From Granby, the railway follows the Colorado River for over 320 kilometres (199 miles) through a series of majestic canyons with impressively formed and coloured rock formations often towering over the line. Many of them can be seen only from the railway, and river-rafters sometimes battle the waters near the centre of Glenwood Springs where the legendary gunslinger and part-time dentist 'Doc' Holliday ended his days. The 1904 stone-and-brick station has two square towers with curious oriental-style roofs.

Dramatic landscapes of mountains and mesas continue to the confluence of the Colorado and Gunnison rivers at Grand Junction, and beyond orchards and vineyards soften the views. After Ruby Canyon, the Colorado River and railway finally part company as the train makes for the sandy Utah Desert. To the north are Book Cliffs, made up of sandstone and shale and resembling the piled-up spines of books.

Westbound freights in steam days would take on a helper at Helper for the climb to Soldier Summit in the Wasatch Mountains. The Old Helper Hotel building includes the Western Mining and Railroad Museum. The sentinel-like rock formations to the north are Castle Gate, where in 1897 Butch Cassidy is said to have relieved the Pleasant Valley Coal Company of $7,000.

A series of horseshoe curves drops the railway down from Soldier Summit with fine views over the snow-capped Wasatch range. After the Mormon centres of Provo and Salt Lake City, the train skirts the Great Salt Lake and then crosses the Nevada Desert salt flats to reach the ranching town of Elko.

Wagon trains heading west in the 1850s crossed the Humboldt River at Winnemucca and paused before crossing the Sierra Nevada. As late as 1900, Butch Cassidy and the Hole in the Wall Gang held up a bank in the town, making off with $2,000 in gold coins.

The Truckee River valley brings the railway to Sparks and the contiguous city of Reno, where rivets were first used to secure men's trouser pockets, an idea patented in 1873 by one

Levi Strauss. Because the next 160 kilometres (100 miles) on to Colfax were the most difficult and costly to build on the whole Union Pacific route, it is not surprising that they offer the finest views from the line, though from the beginning many have been hidden by snow sheds or tunnels through the Sierras.

A place in history was assured for the first station west of Reno, Verdi, by being the scene of one of the first US train robberies, and the first in Nevada, in November 1870. Five men boarded the train and after departure managed to uncouple the express and mail car immediately behind the locomotive from the rest of the train, forcing the train crew at gunpoint to continue further east for 9.6 kilometres (6 miles), where they stopped at an obstruction placed on the track by an accomplice before making off with $41,000 in gold coins. Immediate rewards were offered for the robbers, and they were soon caught and convicted.

Just over the border in California, Truckee once had a magnificent 24-stall roundhouse built of Rocklin granite in 1884, and the town was used as a set in Charlie Chaplin's 1925 film *The Gold Rush*.

The Donner Pass is notorious for snow and provided a challenge for the Central Pacific, but it was already well known throughout the USA for the tragic events of 1846–7, when a group of pioneers left Independence, Missouri, for California, taking a route that roughly paralleled the future transcontinental line. Early snowfall trapped them near what is now called Donner Lake, driving them to cannibalism; only 48 of the 87 members of the party reached California.

The line twists through the mountains and has been the most difficult and costly section of the transcontinental line to improve and provide a second track. There are magnificent views to the south from the train, over the American River

Canyon, and the steep descent is palpable as the train drops down from the Sierras.

The area around Colfax is known for its pears, Hungarian prunes and Tokay grapes, and was named after Vice-President Schuyler Colfax (1823–85), who was one of only two Americans to have held that position and had been a Speaker of the House of Representatives.

The end of the original transcontinental line was California's state capital, Sacramento. Old Sacramento has many fine historic buildings as well as the famous Sutter's Fort, begun in 1839. Railway-connected buildings include the house of the Central Pacific's president, Leland Stanford, with daily tours, but it is the outstanding California State Railroad Museum that is the great draw.

The train flies across flat agricultural land as though impatient to reach the terminus. Davis has a fine 1913 adobe-style station, and the town claims to be the most bike-friendly place in the USA, with more bikes than cars and a university campus closed to automobiles. Suisun Bay and its repository of redundant shipping can be seen in the distance as the train crosses the Carquinez Strait Bridge of 1930 with a lifting span over the shipping channel. After crossing the 1,708-metre (1,868-yard) bridge, the Zephyr skirts San Pablo Bay and then San Francisco Bay to reach Richmond and the first Bay Area Rapid Transit (BART) trains.

Across the bay is the San Francisco skyline and the Golden Gate Bridge, providing a magnificent conclusion to the journey, which ends at Emeryville for the coach transfer into San Francisco.

How long: 51 hours 15 minutes

NARROW GAUGE IN COLORADO

Colorado was *the* state for narrow-gauge railroads. Its 3-foot (914 mm) gauge Denver & Rio Grande Railroad was the longest and most important of the United States' narrow-gauge railroads, but was by no means the only one in the state. Two spectacular and wonderfully authentic heritage railways capture the essence of those railroads, which always had a frontier, 'seat of the pants' atmosphere: the 102-kilometre (63-mile) Cumbres & Toltec Scenic Railroad between Antonito and Chama; and the 72-kilometre (45-mile) Durango & Silverton Narrow Gauge Railroad. Both use steam locomotives and some rolling stock that originally operated over the lines, and both preserve the charm of narrow-gauge railroading.

Freight from mining, timber and livestock were the lifeblood of the railways, though there was a swansong connected with oil and gas drilling in the 1950s. Before the days of the Model T Ford, there had been substantial passenger traffic too. Besides the miners, stockmen and travellers, there were the silver kings, for whom sleeping cars on night trains and luxury parlour cars on day trains were attached. The river bed of the Animas River was said to be littered with champagne and vintage Cognac bottles.

Durango station dates from 1882, while the characteristic 15-stall roundhouse for locomotives and a museum was put up in 1989 to replace the original destroyed by fire. The engineer gives two long blasts on the whistle and sets the bell ringing. As steam enters the bulbous cylinders, the ten-coach train eases out of the depot, as Americans call their railway stations.

This is a good moment to enjoy pastries and a beverage from the Caboose Coffee Shop, because the flat exit from Durango alongside Highway 550 isn't the most exciting prelude to one of the world's great rail journeys. But things look up from the moment the train stops beside the water tank at Hermosa for the locomotive to slake its thirst and prepare for the climb, which continues almost without respite all the way to Silverton, high in the San Juan Mountains at 2,840 metres (9,318 feet). There are views over Shalona Lake before Beaver Creek Canyon and some red granite cuttings at Rockwood.

For much of the way, the railway snakes along a shelf high above the Animas River on a section known appropriately as the High Line, with an almost sheer drop to the water over 120 metres (394 feet) below. Conifers line the opposite slope of the canyon, which narrows and then widens for an unexpected meadow and groves of aspens with their shimmering leaves that change from pale green to yellow to red in autumn.

Railway and river come alongside one another before the valley suddenly opens out on the approach to Silverton, where the trains stop close to the centre, designated a National Historic Landmark District and full of period buildings such as the splendid Grand Imperial Hotel with its tin-stamped ceilings. The last mine closed in 1991, so the town depends on tourism and the railway, which has featured in such films as *How the West Was Won* and *Butch Cassidy and the Sundance Kid*.

The Cumbres & Toltec Scenic Railroad has also starred in numerous feature films. Its survival owes much to the farsightedness of the states of Colorado and New Mexico, which jointly purchased the railway, structures and nine steam locomotives after the line closed to commercial

Photo: Milan Savajac

traffic in 1969. Its operation is in the hands of an interstate agency, the Cumbres & Toltec Scenic Railroad Commission, supported by a not-for-profit membership organisation that focuses on interpretation and conservation of the railway's historic assets and character.

The scenery on the Cumbres & Toltec is no less impressive, thanks to the climb through sheep-ranching country, forest and immense outcrops of volcanic rock to the 3,053-metre (10,016-foot) summit at Cumbres Pass. Aspen woods give way to conifers, and deer, elk and occasionally bears can be seen. The line crosses many trestle bridges and has to describe such tight loops that locomotive and the last carriage can be travelling in opposite directions on long trains.

At the isolated midway point of Osier, passengers tuck into a turkey or meatloaf lunch in a dining-hall added to the station and section house in 1979. A cache of coal was kept at Osier in case of emergencies and for the rotary snowplough that battled to keep the line open. Continuing after lunch, the train reaches the narrow Toltec Gorge, edging along a shelf above the deep canyon below. A curious memorial beside the line marks the spot where an impromptu memorial service was held in 1881 when passengers learned of the assassination of President James Garfield after little more than six months at the White House.

Gradually the train descends among gentler hills softened by aspens to a broad plain of sagebrush and the terminus at Antonito.

How long: 7 hours 30 minutes

SUNSET LIMITED (ORLANDO–LOS ANGELES)

The Sunset Limited is the oldest continuously used train name in the USA, having been introduced as the Sunset Express, an all-Pullman train, by the Southern Pacific Railroad in 1894 between San Francisco and New Orleans. Today linking Orlando and Los Angeles, the Sunset Limited is the most southerly of the long-distance trains run by Amtrak, a corporation that has operated it since 1971.

On leaving the 1954-built Union station in New Orleans, the distinctive shape of the Superdome dominates the view, invoking memories of Hurricane Katrina, when the 70,000-plus stadium became a refuge of last resort. As the train heads into the suburbs, it clatters over the longest railroad bridge in the USA, the 7.2-kilometre-long (4.5-mile) Huey P. Long Bridge, named after a popular governor who advocated radical action to cure the ills of the Depression. Much good it did him; he was assassinated in 1935. The bridge's matrix of steel girders looks endless. Below is the bend in the Mississippi River that gives the city one of its nicknames, the Crescent City. Trains crossed the river by ferry until the bridge was opened in 1935.

Alligator-infested bayous lined with moss-covered oaks and cypress trees give way to the sugar-cane fields around New Iberia which feed into the town's Sugar Cane Festival in September. Venerable oak trees shade the historic downtown area. Bayous are crossed on causeways and trestles, and the trappings of offshore oil and gas rigs periodically intrude on the passing scenes, while the salt dome of Avery Island, ringed by bayous, is the famous source of Tabasco sauce.

Stately mansions dot the Louisiana sugar-cane fields

before arrival in the 'capital of Arcadiana' at Lafayette, home to descendants of the Cajuns who fled Nova Scotia. The crayfish that headline so many Cajun and Creole dishes share with rice the flooded fields beside the line, and they feature in the many restaurants of Lafayette.

As the border with Texas is crossed east of Orange, it's a salutary thought that a day later the train is still trundling through the Lone Star state. Orange is a deep-water port on the Gulf of Mexico and part of a major industrial area based on oil, which was first discovered in 1901 at nearby Spindletop. The industrial character continues at Beaumont, home to the legendary athlete Mildred 'Babe' Didrikson Zaharias who set two world records in the 1932 Olympics.

Houston is the fourth largest city in the USA and has an impressive skyline, but San Antonio is the better place to choose for a break in the journey with its historic downtown district, the Alamo and the River Walk of restaurants, bars and shops. The historic Fairmount Hotel of 1906 is one of the largest structures ever moved; in 1985 it was eased on rollers for five blocks to its current site in La Villita National Historic District.

After rain, pistachio trees provide splashes of green among the rolling hills of western Texas as the train heads into prairie country and the climb towards New Mexico. West of Del Rio is a spectacular crossing of the Pecos River canyon on the High Bridge, and far to the south can be seen the town of Langtry. This was home to 'Judge' Roy Bean who held court in his own saloon, which he named the Jersey Lillie because of his admiration for the British actress and courtesan Lillie Langtry. The town's name was a coincidence; it was named after a railroad engineer, George Langtry.

The landscape becomes steadily more barren, the arid ground strewn with prickly pear, monumental cacti and the yucca, Spanish dagger. Classic country for a train robbery, which is what happened in 1912 when two masked men – one from Butch Cassidy's Hole in the Wall Gang – staged the last train robbery in Texas.

Some passengers may detrain at Alpine to visit Big Bend National Park, bordered by the Rio Grande and known for its geology and palaeontology. The climb continues through barren lands of cactus to the highest point on the route, the 1,545-metre (5,069-foot) summit at Paisano Pass in the Del Norte Mountains. Orchards of pecan trees and the encircling Franklin Mountains herald the suburbs of El Paso, so extensive that the largest urban park in the USA, of 9,712 hectares (23,998 acres) is entirely within the city limits. The Coen brothers used the city to shoot *No Country for Old Men*. The first Hilton high-rise hotel was built here, in 1930, but it is the 1905–6 railway station that deserves attention; it was designed by the same architect as that of Union station in Washington, Daniel Burnham.

The railway leaves the Lone Star State and enters New Mexico at a crossing of the Rio Grande, and the railway comes within 9 metres (30 feet) of the Mexican border. The landscape becomes quintessential Wild West country, and the hawk-eyed passenger may spot both rattlesnakes, warming themselves on trackside lava rock from an extinct volcano, and 'Window Peak', a hole through a ridge in the Florida Mountains. This is country associated with the Mexican revolutionary Pancho Villa and Billy the Kid.

Between Deming and Lordsburg, the continental divide is reached at 1,398 metres (4,587 feet) shortly before crossing into Arizona and what was once Apache country. It was in the Peloncillo Mountains that Chief Geronimo surrendered to the US cavalry in 1886, bringing an end to the Indian Wars. Before reaching Tucson, hundreds of aircraft stored

Photo: Clay Gilliland

in the dry desert climate can be seen to the north of the line. Tucson was established as a Spanish fort in 1775, and thanks to the five surrounding mountain ranges its movie studio was the setting and base for over 300 westerns.

A converted California Zephyr dome car stands beside the station at Maricopa. By the time the train reaches the popular tourist resort of Yuma on the Colorado River, the railway is in the Sonoran Desert, renowned for its sand dunes and for being the wettest desert on earth. Eucalyptus trees herald the final state line, as the train enters California and the first stop at Palm Springs. This desert city is also a popular resort, famous with tennis-players and golfers, and has a 4-kilometre (2.5-mile) cablecar to give panoramic views over the Coachella Valley.

Giant windmills generating green electricity flank the track as the train heads through Ontario, where Maglites are made, and Pomona before reaching the suburbs of Los Angeles. The huge complexes of the California State University and LA County Hospital are passed before arrival at Union station, opened in 1939 in a marriage of Spanish and Art Deco styles and the last of the great 'union' stations to be built, bringing all passenger services into a single hub. Tinseltown awaits.

How long: 44 hours 30 minutes–47 hours 45 minutes

COPPER CANYON (MEXICO)

There was little railway building during the second half of the 20th century, but an extraordinary railway in northern

Mexico was an exception. Though construction began at the beginning of the century, it was not completed until 1961. The 651-kilometre (405-mile) Ferrocarril Chihuahua al Pacifico links the hot inland industrial city of Chihuahua and the town of Los Mochis on the Gulf of California and traverses terrain that is anything but conducive to railway building. So remarkable are the mountain landscapes and gorges that the El Chepe, as the train is called, has become a major tourist attraction. There are two trains a day: the limited-stop *primera* with bar and restaurant car, and the slower *economica*, which stops everywhere and has a snack car.

Mexicans who know any history revere Chihuahua as the place where a radical priest named Manuel Hidalgo began the revolt against the Spanish yoke in 1811. It was also home to another revolutionary, Pancho Villa, who has been portrayed in dozens of films; Raoul Walsh, Yul Brunner and Antonio Banderas are among those who have played him. A museum in the city is devoted to his exploits, which included invading the USA.

Curiously, Chihuahua's signature is not tiny dogs with irritating barks but Stetsons rather than sombreros. The fertile land of Chihuahua state is evident during the first flat stretch after leaving Chihuahua Pacific station: agriculture dominates, emphasised by the grain and maize silos at Fresno. At Santa Isabel the train joins the river of the same name to wind into low hills and a rock-walled river canyon. The first of 87 tunnels is burrowed as the train climbs steeply in a series of loops to a plateau of apple and peach orchards and the adobe station of Anáhuac. Many of the farmers are Mennonites of Dutch and German ancestry who had migrated first from Russia to Manitoba and then in the 1920s to Mexico. By 1927 about 7,000 Canadian Mennonites lived in Mexico, principally in Chihuahua state.

Photo: Interspectrum

La Junta is a railway town and junction for a line north to Juarez. Farms alternate with rugged river valleys, which steepen as the railway finally gets to grips with the mountains that have been visible in the distance for much of the journey. There are places where a viaduct straddles a valley and towers over forest resembling broccoli florets. Pine-wooded slopes feed periodic sawmills, but the logging centre of Creel has become a popular overnight stop for tourists wanting to visit nearby canyons and waterfalls. Creel has been the location for Westerns starring John Wayne among others, but today it lives off tourism and has souvenir shops aplenty selling crafts made by the indigenous Tarahumaras Indians who rival Kenyan Kalenjins for prowess as runners, though the Mexicans are known for endurance rather than speed.

The climb continues to the 2,460-metre (8,071-foot) summit at Los Ojitos and the descent by a full spiral to Divisadero, where there is a 15-minute stop for passengers to admire the Copper Canyon. Combined with the adjoining Urique Canyon, the Copper Canyon is four times larger than the Grand Canyon and derives its name from both mining operations and the colour of the rock. The chasm is 1,000 metres (3,281 feet) deep and stretches for 640 kilometres (398 miles) through the Sierra Madre mountains. It was formed by volcanic activity rather than river erosion. A single hotel stands precariously on the edge of a cliff, and guests can watch eagles glide and hummingbirds flit from tree to tree.

On the descent, the train passes adobe brickmaking and more sawmills and leaps over gullies and valleys on a succession of girder bridges. After numerous tunnels comes one of the scenic and engineering highlights in the great loop at Santa Barbara in a ring of mountains. Though dropping down, the railway is still among impressive mountains with waterfalls and rock summits protruding above the green slopes, some steep enough to require avalanche shelters over the railway.

The terrain changes to scrubby desert with cactus and mesquite trees, and some passengers detrain at El Fuerte, a colonial town founded in 1564, because the remainder of the line to Los Mochis is relatively uninteresting.

How long: 14 hours

TREN CRUCERO (ECUADOR)

The Andes posed a greater challenge to railway builders than any other mountain range; other ranges were more extensive, but until the railway reached Tibet none exceeded the Andes for the height the tracks had to climb. Moreover, the projected traffic often forced promoters to adopt wider gauges than the 2 feet 6 inches (762 mm) used for the hill station railways of India, for example, thereby increasing the cost and limiting the options of the surveyors and civil engineers.

Like so many South American railways, the construction of the line that eventually linked Ecuador's principal port of Guayaquil with its political capital, Quito, was subject to all manner of vicissitudes: difficulty raising capital; false starts requiring a change of gauge; trouble recruiting enough workers, who were then afflicted by pestilence; riots; assassination; and all the obstacles that the terrain and climate could summon.

Opening of the 452-kilometre (281-mile) line in 1908, 37 years after construction began, was largely the achievement of two Virginian brothers: Archer Harman was the guiding spirit and 'fixer', while the West Point graduate Major John Harman was the engineer. They built the 3-foot 6-inch (1,067 mm) gauge railway under the auspices of the Guayaquil & Quito Railway Company, which was incorporated in New Jersey and largely financed by British capital.

For over half a century the railway carried out its promoters' intention of forming the transport backbone of the country, but construction of faster roads gradually eroded traffic. By the last quarter of the 20th century, the diesel *autoferro* railcar or carriages hauled by the railway's Philadelphia-built steam locomotives had become a 'must-do' for more adventurous tourists, preferably riding on the roof. Ducking one's head through the tunnels was an obvious precaution, but an unfortunate contretemps between a wire and the neck of a Japanese roof-rider put paid to the fun.

The railway became almost moribund through lack of investment, but in 2008 President Correa committed $245 million to rebuilding the railway for domestic and inbound tourism. Local communities would benefit from facilities created in station buildings, such as craft shops, cafés and meeting spaces, as well as local train services. The flagship air-conditioned Tren Crucero (Cruise Train) is made up of a bar car with banquettes, open cars with armchairs at tables, and another lounge car with open rear veranda. Meals during the four-day itinerary are taken in restaurants or haciendas and guests sleep in hotels or haciendas.

Travelling west to east not only provides a greater sense of climax, but also provides a gradual acclimatisation to the altitude. Departure from Guayaquil is now from a smart new two-storey station, a world away from the ramshackle wooden building that passed for a station in the 1980s. A steam locomotive often hauls the train over the flat coastal section, easing the train away from the station along a palm-lined road between an anarchic mélange of concrete, breeze blocks, wires and reinforcing bars reaching for the sky.

As the train strikes out across the delta of the Guayas River, reedy marshes give way to a mosaic of rice paddies with mud walls graced by egrets. Split-cane houses roofed with corrugated iron stand on spindly poles to protect them from flooding and unwelcome creatures, and fields of sugar cane are patrolled by hawks and red-headed vultures.

The first of the off-train excursions using a shadowing coach or on foot is to the cacao plantation of San Rafael for a taste of the sweet white pulp that surrounds the beans before they are fermented and dried and sent off to make some of the world's finest chocolate. An atmospheric walk into Cloud Forest, renowned for their biodiversity, completes the first day.

The climb from Bucay on the second day is one of the toughest in the world: in just 77 kilometres (48 miles) the railway ascends from 294 metres above sea level (965 feet) to 3,239 metres (10,627 feet). It does this by gradients at the limit of adhesion even for a powerful diesel locomotive and by one of the great railway wonders of the world – the Devil's Nose zig-zag. The mountain known as Pistishi, or the Condor's Nest by the local Indians, blocked the passage of the railway. Its shape and the difficulties it caused gave rise to the name that has stuck – La Nariz del Diablo. Along its near perpendicular cliffs, a ledge for the railway was hacked and blasted by the largely Jamaican and Ecuadorian workforce under the guidance of John Harman. By 1901 trains were able to charge up the first arm of the switchback before reversing up the second and again changing direction for the third arm, facing the 'right' way.

From Bucay the railway runs alongside the Chanchán

Photo: amalavida.tv

River, whose raging waters had destroyed long sections of the line before reconstruction on a less vulnerable alignment. The wooded valley gradually narrows, forcing the railway over frequent river crossings to find a route between slopes etched with ravines, some offering a glimpse of the arc of a waterfall fed by springs on distant summits.

Built before road traffic, the railway often runs along the centre of main streets, and at Huigra it passes between the two-storey houses and a statue commemorating Eloy Alfaro, the president whose determination created the railway but who, like so many early South American presidents, met an unpleasant end. So did 190 track workers when they were buried by an avalanche in 1931, the spot marked by a cross above Huigra.

The veranda is packed for the ascent of the Devil's Nose. The audacity of building a railway up the mountain and the steepness of the slopes rising far out of sight above the line astonish even seasoned rail travellers. The train winds round the bridge of the 'nose' to reach the upper level and heads along a bucolic valley of eucalyptus trees, introduced from Australia by President Moreno in the 19th century to try to stabilise the hillsides. The valley broadens out to allow the train to describe two great horseshoe loops on the climb to Alausi, dominated by a colossal painted statue of the town's patron saint, St Peter.

Pines introduced from California add variety to the vegetation as the train climbs the Cordillera Occidental range, pausing for a visit to a Belgian-supported educational centre in Guamote and the oldest church in Ecuador built by the Spaniards in 1534 at Balbanera, all dark stone, tiny windows and gaudy Madonnas.

At Riobamba the train reverses into the station for the second night, as light fades on the crown of snow on the dormant summit of Chimborazo at 6,268 metres (20,564 feet). This mountain is depicted in one of America's most famous paintings, *The Heart of the Andes*, by Connecticut-born Frederic Church; now in the Metropolitan Museum of Art in New York, when it was first exhibited in the city over 12,000 people queued to see it and hand over 25¢ for the privilege. Chimborazo was first climbed by the English mountaineer Edward Whymper in 1880, and its conquest placed him closer to the sun than anyone before him, since Chimborazo lies on the equatorial bulge, making it further from the Earth's centre than even Mount Everest.

The climb resumes on the third day to reach the line's summit. Leaving Riobamba, and in common with countless other developing-country towns, it is easy to get the measure of stray dogs and their temperament from the train; dogs' reactions to the train range from nonchalant indifference to a furious sense of trespass on their territory and a noisy chase of the iron monster, which is always seen off the premises to allow a look of self-satisfaction.

Few stations have been built at such a lonely spot as Urbina, the highest station on the line, at 3,609 metres (11,841 feet). Sheltered by a few trees and a couple of railway houses, the station building has been turned into a hostel for walkers and climbers on Chimborazo. The panorama over surrounding mountains is spectacular, often ringed by wreaths of cloud below their summits. The line descends through landscapes reminiscent of the Scottish lowlands, dropping down into the deep basin filled by the city of Ambato, which had to be rebuilt after it was levelled by an earthquake in 1949.

The final night is spent within two-metre-thick walls of volcanic rock in one of the country's most historic haciendas. The destruction of the Spanish Armada was eight years away when Hacienda Cienega was built in 1580, and its dark rooms and corridors overlooking the courtyard garden are redolent of times when power rested with a landed elite. Visitors with a suitable prefix – Marshal, Count or Don – were welcomed, and Baron Alexander von Humboldt stayed here while he was studying nearby Cotopaxi in 1802. Crude portraits of long-forgotten Spaniards hang beneath stone vaults, and the entrance is aligned with one of the country's oldest avenues of eucalyptus, the upper branches meeting overhead like a Gothic nave.

It's pot luck whether the vagaries of mountain weather allow a clear view of Cotopaxi's symmetrical white cone with its apex reaching 5,897 metres (19,347 feet). The mountain inspired another of Church's most famous paintings, *Cotopaxi*, now in Detroit, and fine views of the mountain can be had from the train as it bowls along what Humboldt called 'the Avenue of Volcanoes'.

The journey through seven of the country's nine climatic zones ends in the well-restored station compound at Quito. It's a measure of the regard people have for the railway and their station that here – in the oldest capital of the Americas and a World Heritage Site – Quiteños voted the railway station their favourite building. President Correa must have been gratified.

How long: 4 days

LIMA–HUANCAYO (PERU)

The Central of Peru from Lima to Huancayo is not a journey for the faint-hearted or those prone to altitude sickness

– until the Chinese built the Qingzang Railway to Lhasa, it took you as high as you could reach on a service train. Nor is it the easiest train to catch; despite being one of the most awe-inspiring railways in the world, there is only one train a month and you have to spend two or three nights at Huancayo waiting for the return working or travel on over even more terrifying Andean roads.

But this 'audacious marvel of engineering science', as one early writer put it, is worth the effort. The first to recognise that a railway was necessary to realise the potential of the mineral deposits in the *cordillera* was the Cornishman Richard Trevithick. He acted as a consultant to the mines of Cerro de Pasco during the late 1810s, interrupted by service in Simon Bolivar's army. But the man who converted Trevithick's dream into reality was the American buccaneering entrepreneur and engineer Henry Meiggs.

After building railways in Chile, he moved on to Peru, but as Brian Fawcett, son of the mysteriously lost Andean explorer Col. Percy Fawcett, wrote, 'beside the Central of Peru, all other Andean systems are child's play!' Those operating the Guayaquil & Quito line in Ecuador might demur from this assessment, but no other railway had to compress a higher climb into so few miles – ascending 4,782 metres (15,689 feet) in 170 kilometres (106 miles).

In the absence of almost unlimited capital for tunnelling and monumental viaducts, the only way to construct a line in valleys too narrow for horseshoe curves was to use the zig-zag or switchback; this allows a train to proceed into a headshunt, reverse up the hillside to another dead-end and then proceed on another rising track. The idea dates from the 1840s, when it was used on a coal line in Pennsylvania and on the Ithaca & Oswego Railroad in New York, but its first main line application was at the Bhore Ghat on the

Photo: Rabelleger / David Gubler

Great Indian Peninsula Railway from Bombay to Poona, which opened in 1863.

Construction of the standard-gauge Central of Peru began in 1870 and 141 kilometres (88 miles) to Chicla had been built by the time war with Chile halted work in 1878. Meiggs had died the previous year, so the baton was handed to a Polish engineer, Ernest Malinowski, and then to John L. Thorndike of Franklin County, New York. Not until 1908 were services to Huancayo inaugurated; financial problems, disease among the workforce and accidents had added to the engineering difficulties and prolonged construction.

Trains leave from the neo-classical Desamparados station of 1912, which has a fussy grandeur and an art nouveau skylight. It is a truism of the western cordillera that if it is raining on the coast, it is likely to be sunny inland, and vice versa. Platform vendors outnumber passengers climbing into the recently refurbished carriages with roof windows and better seats. Oxygen supplies and attendants are on hand to help those overcome by the thinning air.

The locomotive's horn blares constantly as the train forges through the nether world of the *barrios* before reaching fields of cotton, maize and alfalfa. The railway follows the River Rímac – in Quechua 'the water that speaks' – for the first 155 kilometres (96 miles) as far as Ticlio. Though there isn't a metre of track that isn't climbing, it is easy going until Chosica, where the pleasant climate has made it a favoured place for wealthier families to escape from Lima.

Leaving Chosica, there are still green fields splashed against the brown slopes, growing fruit and vegetables, but a deeper growl from the locomotive emphasises a sudden change in character as the real climb begins. The first of 67 tunnels precedes the first of eleven reversing points at Tornamesa, unique in being a single reverse – a V rather than a Z. From here the gradient is seldom less than 1 in 25 all the way to the continental divide inside the summit tunnel through Mount Meiggs.

At San Bartolomé the line crosses the Rímac and the houses roofed in green and red corrugated iron along the valley floor soon look Lilliputian as the train climbs to the Verrugas Gorge and the railway's tallest and longest viaduct, Carrión Bridge. It was named after Dr Daniel Carrión, who died after injecting himself with the infected blood of a railway worker as part of his efforts to find the cause of a fever so virulent that it is estimated to have killed 7,000 construction workers. The 175-metre-long (574-foot) bridge stands 77 metres (253 feet) above the canyon and is the third on the site, built by the Cleveland Bridge & Engineering Company of Darlington in 1937.

Gasps of astonishment are often the only sound from passengers as they marvel at the dizzying drops from bridges and the sheer scale of the mountain landscape unfolding with the climb. The railway is cut into an almost vertical wall of rock; workers creating the ledge had to be suspended from baskets on ropes. Giant cacti have been the usual flora, but at Matucana there is grass good enough for cattle. Flatcars loaded with milk churns used to begin a gravity descent to Lima from the station, but accidents were so frequent that the service was stopped.

The terrain becomes more inhospitable and arid, though there are signs of the hillside having been terraced for agriculture. The sheer walls and narrowness of some defiles prevent the sun ever reaching some parts. Beyond the first double reverse at Viso is the Chaupichaca Bridge, where a runaway locomotive collided with a crane renewing a span in 1909, sending 200 men and a pile of wreckage into the river below. The remains of the wreckage can still be seen.

Tamboraque station is the start of another zig-zag and series of tunnels. Blink and you could miss the Infiernillo Bridge that links two tunnels. By Cacray there are few trees but many screes, and efforts to prevent landslides by planting trees along the line have largely failed. Near the upper reversal at Cacray is the old *Camino Real*, the Royal Road, along which the gold and silver from the mines was carried to the coast before the railway was built.

Rio Blanco is where some passengers start to feel the effects of altitude, though most experience nothing more than slight breathlessness. Chicla was the railhead for 14 years while the Peruvian economy languished following its unsuccessful war against Chile, forcing the government to concede mining and other rights, including the railways, to American and British creditors.

The first sign of mining operations appears at Bellavista, and soon after Casapalca there is a great horseshoe loop and a change in direction to reach the isolated passing loop named after Meiggs, surrounded by peaks. Snow banks drape the gullies and peaks at even the warmest times of year. After more vertigo-inducing drops and eight tunnels, the train arrives at Ticlio, a cold, rather depressing place and until the 21st century the highest junction in the world, for a mineral branch to Morococha.

Just beyond Ticlio station is the northern portal of the longest tunnel on the line, Galera at 2.1 kilometres (6,890 feet). Fawcett told of an important American who asked for the train to be stopped at the summit inside the tunnel marking the continental divide. He got down and returned after a few minutes, saying 'There! I have fulfilled a great ambition. I have watered the Atlantic and Pacific oceans simultaneously.'

The descent down the eastern slopes of the *cordillera* is less dramatic, and after the final and only zig-zag on the Atlantic side, the valley broadens. La Oroya is the junction for the railway to the mines of Cerro de Pasco, which were a major source of William Randolph Hearst's wealth. Astonishingly, since 1817 the mines had used four winding and four high-pressure steam pumping engines designed by Trevithick and made in Cornwall, which had been shipped out in kit form the previous year, hauled into the Andes by mules and assembled at the mines by four Cornishmen.

The character of the landscape changes again as the mines are left behind and the train reaches an upland area of pastoral and cereal farms sheltered by belts of eucalyptus. The railway follows the River Mantaro all the way to journey's end, and at wayside stations Indian women in broad-rimmed stovepipe hats board the train to buy or sell in the market at Huancayo.

How long: 14 hours

TRAIN TO THE CLOUDS (ARGENTINA–CHILE)

One of the last railway lines to be completed in South America was the Northern Transandine linking Salta in northern Argentina with the Chilean port of Antofagasta. The idea of a railway between the cities was mooted as early as 1889, but construction work began only in 1921 and the whole railway was not opened until 20 February 1948.

The metre-gauge (3 feet 3 inches) railway was engineered by Philadelphia-born Richard Maury, who became one of Argentina's foremost railway engineers and a professor at

Photo: Véronique Debord-Lazaro

the University of Tucamán. He was buried at the foot of a monument at Campo Quijano station on the route of the Tren a las Nubes (Train to the Clouds).

The tourist Tren a las Nubes operates over the section of line from Salta in northern Argentina for 217 kilometres (135 miles) to La Polvorilla Viaduct at 4,220 metres (13,845 feet), close to the line's summit at Chorrillos at 4,475 metres (14,682 feet). The bar car even serves maté de coca to ward off altitude sickness, but nurses are also on hand for the more universal antidote of a whiff of oxygen. It leaves from General Belgrano station in Salta and strides across fields of tobacco, sugar cane and cattle with a gaucho or two in attendance. Breakfast of sweet croissants and coffee is served before Campo Quijano.

The train negotiates 29 bridges, 21 tunnels, thirteen viaducts, two spirals and two zig-zags on its course through arid canyons of cacti and on to the equally dry altiplano, dotted with mostly abandoned adobe houses. The only town en route is San Antonio de los Cobres, which once flourished on the back of copper mining but today wears a desolate air with some boarded-up houses, though it has a modern hotel near the station.

Lunch in the dining car can be bought before the train crosses the arc of La Polvorilla Viaduct and terminates at a run-round loop, giving passengers about half an hour for a gentle stroll in the thin air and to take pictures of the 224-metre-long (735 feet), 70 metre-high (230 feet) viaduct. The railway continues for freight only, reaching the border with Chile at Socompa after another 352 kilometres (219 miles).

The line beyond the viaduct passes through country rich in mineral resources, such as lead, copper and lithium, which remain largely untapped, partly due to poor transport links. Talks have been held to reopen the line to exploit these minerals. If the tourist train seems rather tame, there is the option of riding a weekly freight train with a passenger coach or two to the border, where, in theory, it is possible to catch a Chilean freight train to the Pacific.

How long: 16 hours

APPENDIX:
TICKETS AND INFORMATION

Belmond (0845 077 2222; belmond.com) operates the Venice Simplon Orient-Express, the Royal Scotsman, British Pullman, Northern Belle and Grand Hibernian.

Ffestiniog Travel (01766 772030; ffestiniogtravel.com) offers a programme of escorted tours with general rail and cultural travel, tram and enthusiast themes in Europe and North America. It also sells rail tickets and passes for many countries, and its profits support the Ffestiniog and Welsh Highland railways.

Golden Eagle Luxury Trains (0161 928 9410; goldeneagleluxurytrains.com) operates the Golden Eagle Trans-Siberian Express and Danube Express tourist trains.

Great Rail Journeys (0800 140 4444; greatrail.com) is a guided and independent rail-based holiday specialist covering all continents.

Inside Track (01296 714823; railwayholidays.com) operates a range of escorted UK and European tours with an emphasis on nostalgic transport and scenic and cultural attractions.

Luxury Train Club (01249 890205; luxurytrainclub.com) provides a booking and travel service for all luxury trains.

The Man in Seat 61 (seat61.com) provides an unrivalled site for information about train travel worldwide.

PTG Tours (01235 227288; ptg.co.uk) offers escorted enthusiast, general interest and cultural rail tours to countries as far afield as Sri Lanka and New Zealand.

Railbookers (020 3327 1562; railbookers.com) sells independent rail-based holidays on all continents.

Railtrail Tours (01538 382323; railtrail.co.uk) offers a wide programme of UK and European escorted holidays with steam travel to the fore.

The Railway Touring Co (01553 661500; railwaytouring. net) arranges escorted tours using steam wherever possible in the UK, Europe, North and South America, India, Sri Lanka and Japan.

Switzerland Travel Centre (020 7420 4934; stc.co.uk) offer a range of Swiss passes, tickets and hotels.

Trainseurope (0871 700 7722; trainseurope.co.uk) sells train tickets and passes for Europe and North America.

Trans-Siberian Travel Company (020 8816 8925; thetranssiberiantravelcompany.com) offers an expert booking service for all Trans-Siberian services.

Voyages-sncf (0844 848 5848; voyages-sncf.com), formerly Rail Europe, sells European rail tickets and passes.

NOTES

NOTES

Also available

PETER
PUGH

MOST INFLUENTIAL
BRITONS
OF THE LAST 100 YEARS

ISBN: 9781785780349 (paperback) / 9781785780356 (ebook)

IN ASSOCIATION WITH
TIMPSON

Also available

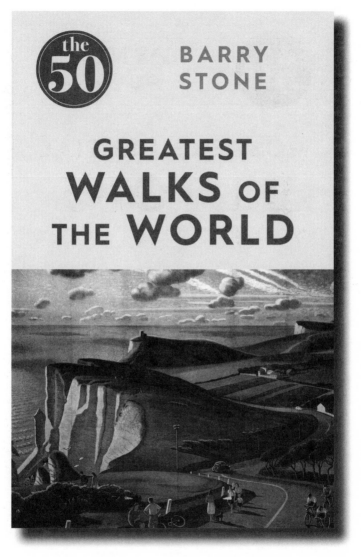

BARRY
STONE

GREATEST
WALKS OF
THE WORLD

ISBN: 9781785780639 (paperback) / 9781785780646 (ebook)

IN ASSOCIATION WITH
TIMPSON

Also available

the
50

STEVEN
WHITE

GREATEST
RUGBY UNION
PLAYERS OF ALL TIME

ISBN: 9781785780264 (paperback) / 9781785780271 (ebook)

IN ASSOCIATION WITH
TIMPSON